Deciduous trees – silhouettes

English Oak

Sessile Oak

Lombardy Poplar

Downy Birch

Silver Birch

Plane

Ash

HarperCollinsPublishers
77–85 Fulham Palace Road
London W6 8JB

www.collins.co.uk ·

Collins is a registered trademark of HarperCollinsPublishers

09 08 07 06 05
11 10 9

ISBN 0 00 219993 9

Originally published in German as a GU Nature Guide by
Gräfe und Unzer GmbH, Munich

Written by Gregor Aas and Andreas Riedmiller
Drawings by Heinz Bogner
This edition translated and adapted by Martin Walters

Translator's acknowledgement:
I should like to thank my father Martin Walters for his advice
and Anne James for her help with typing the translation

Printed and bound in Singapore by Imago

Collins · NATURE GUIDE

TREES
OF BRITAIN & EUROPE

G. Aas • A. Riedmiller

Translated and adapted by
MARTIN WALTERS

Collins

Introduction

This tree guide is designed to enable anyone to identify trees, even the most inexperienced garden visitor. It is handy in format and very light in weight, making it the ideal identification guide for both home and field use. Virtually all native central and northern European trees are illustrated and described, as well as important introduced species, and a selection of the commoner trees of southern Europe and the Mediterranean.

The 800 colour photographs have nearly all been taken specially for this book. They show the whole trees as well as vital details such as needles, leaves, flowers and bark. The text is organised into useful sections and gives concise notes on the important characteristics of each species, as well as information on distribution, habitat and any other important facts.

The colour coding system provides a simple but effective guide to identification, even for those without botanical knowledge. The tree species are divided into 6 groups, each with its own colour code and symbol. The species descriptions with their photographs are grouped together in colour sections, and each section is marked by coloured thumb-markers. The colour and texture of bark (shown on pp. 246–251), and tree silhouettes (inside front and back covers) are additional important guides to identification, especially in winter.

At the back of the book there is a short botanical section with explanations of technical terms, information on tree diseases, and a full species index of common and Latin names.

The authors would like to thank Professor Peter Schütt for his help during the book's preparation, and Mr Heinz Bogner for his impressive tree silhouettes and botanical line drawings.

The tree groups, colour codes and symbols

COLOUR	SYMBOL	TYPE OF TREE	PAGE
		Conifers with needles inserted singly	8–41
		Conifers with needles arranged in bunches, each bunch of 2,3 or 5 needles	42–67
		Conifers with scale-like leaves	68–77
		Broadleaved trees with compound leaves (leaf consisting of several separate leaflets, growing from a common stalk)	78–105
		Broadleaved trees with simple, undivided leaves (leaf-blade entire, but may be lobed). Leaves opposite, always 2 per node	106–127
		Broadleaved trees with simple, undivided leaves (leaf-blade entire, but may be lobed). Leaves alternate, always 1 per node	128–239

Exceptions:

Ginkgo (p. 128) is not a broadleaved tree (in the taxonomic sense; it is a Gymnosperm) but it is in the pale green group since it has simple, broad, alternate leaves.

Alder Buckthorn (p. 118) has alternate leaves but is described as a similar species with Buckthorn, in the dark green (opposite-leaved) group.

Within each colour group the tree species are, with a few exceptions, arranged in systematic order (family, genus).

How to identify a tree

When you have your tree in front of you, first decide to which of the 6 colour groups the tree belongs, then use the colour photographs and diagnostic notes to find the species. Always use the maximum number of features to confirm the identification. Find a typical leaf by selecting it from several, preferably having looked at leaves from more than one branch. Leaves from suckers or other vigorous shoots are often untypical so should not be used for identification.

Coverage of species

This guide includes most European trees and taller shrubs, as well as the most important trees of parks, gardens, and forestry, and a selection of the commoner trees of southern Europe and the Mediterranean.

Explanation of text notes

Trees are individuals, and characters vary, both on a single individual, and between individual specimens of one species. The **colour photographs** can only show the features of one or a few individuals of each species, so there may well be differences between the specimen you wish to identify and its illustration. For this reason it is important to use the information provided in the notes, as well as the illustrations provided, when identifying a specimen.

The **common name** (or names if more than one is commonly used) is followed by the **Latin name** and the name of the family (in brackets).

Shape describes the typical overall form of the tree – whether it is broadleaved (usually deciduous, i.e. losing all its leaves for part of the year) or a conifer (usually evergreen, i.e. remaining in leaf throughout the year), how tall it may grow (under favourable conditions), and the usual shape of the crown and trunk. All these attributes can alter according to environmental conditions, including the kind of soil the tree is growing in, the weather and how protected the tree is.

Details of **shoot** and **buds** are only given when they are necessary for identification.

Needles and **leaves**, by contrast, are reliable identification features, which vary in their position on the shoot, in outline, in the shape of margin, tip and base, in colour, hairiness and type of stalk. Bear in mind that the measurements given are average (with extremes sometimes noted in brackets) and so deviations from these figures are possible.

Other important features are: type, arrangement, structure, shape, colour and size of **flowers** and **fruits**, which can be useful identification features when they are available.

Bark is another character, and one which, unlike flowers and fruits, is visible throughout the year. In many cases young bark, often smooth, may be distinguished from older, rougher bark.

Distribution is the area occupied naturally by a species. If a tree is not native in Europe, this is specially noted (see symbols below), and information on its status (naturalised or planted) is usually given.

Habitat gives information about the ecology of a species, for example: where it commonly grows, which sorts of soil it prefers, whether it does best in shade or more exposed to sunlight, and whether it tends to be badly damaged by frost or drought.

The note on **similar species** gives a short description of species which might be confused with the main species described and illustrated, or refers to a full description elsewhere in the book. Always be aware of possible similar species when seeking to identify a tree.

Notes provide useful information about particular features of the species which are not covered in the rest of the entry.

Further help with identification

The section on **tree biology** at the end of the book (pp. 240–245) explains, in clear and concise language and with the aid of botanical drawings, the basic scientific knowledge required, and the terms used in the species descriptions. The **species index** (pp. 252–255), which contains both English and Latin names, makes it easy to look up a particular tree.

Abbreviations and symbols

ssp.	= subspecies
♂	= male
♀	= female
X	= hybrid (before the Latin species name)
°	= native to British Isles
⊛	= occasionally or commonly planted in British Isles
BI	= British Isles

Silver Fir ☉

Abies alba

(Pine Family)

Shape: Upright coniferous tree to 50 m; crown at first conical and pointed, later a tall column with flattened top ('Stork's nest crown').
Shoot: With grey-brown hairs. *Buds:* Oval, not resinous.
Needles: Inserted into twig with sheath-like base. Grow radially in good light, spreading to either side in shade. 1.5-3.5 cm long, flat, rounded or notched at tip; shiny dark green above, with 2 white longitudinal stripes below. Needles last 8-12 years.
Flowers: May, separate male and female, on previous season's growth in upper crown. Male flowers 2-3 cm long, cylindrical, yellowish, clumped beneath shoot. Female flowers pale green, in upright cones, 2-6 cm long.
Cones: Oct, upright, only in crown; 10-15 cm long, pale brown, with visible bracts. Cones fall from tree when ripe, leaving just the central axis behind (typical of firs).
Bark: Silver-grey, smooth, cracking into small plates (photo p. 246).
Distribution: Mountains of C and S Europe. Widely planted.
Habitat: Middle and upper tree zones (in Alps to 1600 m); often with Beech and Spruce. On all soils, prefers sites with high air humidity and soil moisture. Sensitive to late frosts; extreme shade tree, deep-rooted.
Similar species: Giant Fir (p. 12), Caucasian Fir (p. 10).
Notes: Threatened over much of natural range. Various factors have been implicated, including pressure from deer grazing, unsuitable forestry practice, and pollution. Used as Christmas tree in many parts of Europe (see also Norway Spruce, p. 22).

Twig upper side (l) and lower side (r)

♂ flowers are clustered on the lower side of the twigs (l), ♀ flowers (miniature cones) grow upright on the upper side (r)

Needles of Silver Fir may be up to 12 years old

Silver fir cones (l) fall off when ripe, leaving the central axis (spindle) visible (r)

Caucasian Fir ✤ ☞

Abies nordmanniana

(Pine Family)

Shape: Coniferous tree growing to 60 m where native, to 30 m in Europe.
Shoot: Hairy at first, becoming hairless later. An extra downwardly directed twig often develops from a fourth bud at the tip of the branch.
Buds: Oval, not resinous.
Needles: Dense, radially inserted and pointing forwards on upper side of twig; spreading to either side below, or in shade. 2-3.5 cm long, flattened, rounded or notched at tip, glossy bright green above, with 2 white longitudinal stripes below.
Cones: Sep-Oct, upright, 12-20 cm long, brown, resinous. Bracts visible.
Bark: Photo p. 246.
Distribution: W Caucasus, N Anatolia (E Turkey). Planted in parks in Europe; in British Isles mainly in N and W.
Habitat: Mountains (900-2000 m). Similar soil requirements to Silver Fir. Frost-hardy. Increasingly popular as Christmas tree, as it drops its needles less readily than Spruce.
Similar species: Silver Fir (p. 8).

Branch of Caucasian Fir

Caucasian Fir: ♂ flowers (l); ripening cone showing bracts sticking out (r)

Korean Fir

Abies koreana

(Pine Family)

Shape: Small coniferous tree to 15 m.
Shoot: Sparsely hairy at first, later hairless; somewhat ridged.
Buds: Rounded, slightly resinous.
Needles: Dense and radially arranged on twigs. Only 1-2 cm long, widening slightly towards the tip, which is rounded or notched. Shiny dark green above, chalky white below.
Cones: Oct-Nov, erect, even on young trees; 4-7 cm long; blue-violet when young, brown when ripe; resinous. Bracts visible.
Distribution: Mountains of S Korea. Often planted in gardens. Infrequent in British Isles.
Habitat: Frost-sensitive; tolerant of different soils as long as they are sufficiently moist.

Korean Fir: note radially arranged needles

Giant Fir ✿☞

Abies grandis

(Pine Family)

Shape: Conifer growing to 85 m in native region (largest of all the firs), and to 60 m in Europe (tallest of all trees in British Isles).

Shoot: Covered in fine hairs. *Buds:* Oval, slightly resinous.

Needles: Comb-like, spreading to either side. 2-5 cm long, those above shorter than those below; shiny dark green above, and with 2 white longitudinal stripes below.

Cones: Sep-Oct, upright, 5-10 cm long, brown, bracts not visible.

Bark: Grey-brown with resin blisters, cracked (photo p. 246).

Distribution: NW North America. In Europe in parks, rarely in plantations.

Habitat: Tolerates even poor soils with sufficient moisture; frost hardy, prefers partial shade, deep rooted.

Similar species: Silver Fir (p. 8).

Branch of Giant Fir

Needles of Giant Fir spread out to either side, both above (l) and below (r)

Veitch's Fir

Abies veitchii

(Pine Family)

Shape: Coniferous tree to 25 m tall.

Shoot: Densely covered in short hairs, or hairless. *Buds:* Rounded, resinous.

Needles: Radially arranged on upper surface of twig, spreading to either side below, pointed towards tip of twig. 1-3 cm long, soft, with blunt, notched tip. Shiny green with longitudinal furrow above, 2 chalky white stripes beneath.

Cones: Sep-Oct, erect on all trees; 6-8 cm long; brown; tips of bracts visible.

Bark: Grey, smooth; circular folds around the branch bases.

Distribution: Japan (Hondo Island). Parks in Europe; not common in BI

Habitat: Rainy mountain sites (1300-2500 m); drought-sensitive, frost-hardy; fairly wide soil type tolerance, but dislikes very chalky soils.

Veitch's Fir: On the upper side (l) needles are shiny green, but chalky white below (r)

Veitch's Fir: needles furrowed on upper side and notched at tip

Noble Fir 🐝☞

(Pine Family)

Abies procera

Shape: Coniferous tree growing to 70 m in native region, to 50 m in Europe. Crown at first conical, later broad and towering, with flattened top.

Shoot: Finely hairy. *Buds:* Small, rounded, and slightly resinous.

Needles: Dense and radially arranged above, spreading to either side below, 2-3.5 cm long, the lower 2- mm curving back along twig, at right angles to main line of needle. Rounded at tip, grey-green on both sides.

Cones: Sep-Oct, upright, very large (15-25 cm), brown. Bracts down-curved and protruding.

Bark: Grey or brown, cracked.

Distribution: W North America. In parks in Europe. In BI mainly in N and W, sometimes used in forestry.

Habitat: Rainy mountains (800-1800 m), often on granite; requires rather moist conditions; hardy, but somewhat sensitive to late frosts.

Noble Fir: branch showing dense, grey-green needles and red ♂ flowers

Twig underside with needles twisted along axis (l); cone with long, projecting bracts (r)

Colorado Fir

(Pine Family)

Abies concolor

Shape: Coniferous tree to 40 m tall, with conical top.

Shoot: Hairless. *Buds:* Rounded to oval, small, resinous.

Needles: Loose, curving upwards on upper side of twig, spreading beneath; very long (4-7 cm), soft, rounded at tip and grey-green on both sides.

Cones: Sep-Oct, upright, 7-13 cm long; bracts not visible.

Bark: Grey, at first smooth, with resin blisters, later cracked (photo p. 246).

Distribution: C North America. Decorative tree in Europe. In BI mainly in N and W, not common

Habitat: Mountains (1800-3600 m); hardy; tolerates wide range of conditions, even dry soils.

The needles of the Colorado Fir curve upwards

Colorado Fir twig showing soft, grey-green needles (l); buds (r)

Greek Fir ☞

Abies cephalonica

(Pine Family)

Shape: Conifer to 35 m tall.

Shoot: Hairless. *Buds:* Oval, resinous.

Needles: Inserted radially and brush-like on the twig; 1.5-3 cm long, twisting towards base; stiff, with a sharp, rarely blunt, tip; shiny, dark green above, weakly furrowed, with irregular white bands towards tip; grey-white longitudinal bands on undersides.

Cones: Upright, 12-17 cm long, brown, resinous. Bracts visible.

Bark: Grey, smooth; becoming cracked with age.

Distribution: Greece. Grown in parks in Europe. Not common in BI.

Habitat: Mountains (800-1600 m), often on calcareous soil; only hardy in protected sites, sensitive to late frosts.

Greek Fir: shoot showing stiff, brush-like needles

Greek Fir: shoot (l), cones exuding resin (r)

Spanish Fir

Abies pinsapo Boiss.

(Pine Family)

Shape: Rather drooping conifer to 25 m tall; often bushy in Europe as a result of frost damage.

Shoot: Hairless. *Buds:* Oval, resinous.

Needles: Always densely clustered and radial on the shoot, even under shady conditions. 1-2 cm long, not twisting towards base; stiff, pointed towards the tip but not very sharp; upper surface not furrowed; dark or grey-green..

Cones: Upright, 10-15 cm long, brown. Bracts not visible.

Distribution: S Spain. The native sites now largely destroyed and restricted to small protected remnants (Sierra de las Nievas). Grown in parks in Europe. Not common in BI.

Habitat: Mountains (1000-2000 m); calcareous soils, drought-resistant but very sensitive to frost.

Spanish Fir: shoot (l); male flowers (r)

Shoot of Spanish Fir with stiff, grey-green needles and male flowers

Douglas Fir ❀

Pseudotsuga menziesii

(Pine Family)

Shape: Conifer growing to 100 m in the native region, in Europe to about 50 m (second tallest tree in Britain). Very quick growing.

Crown: At first conical, flattening out with age with the development of irregular horizontal sturdy branches.

Buds: About 1 cm long, brown, with conical tips.

Needles: Radial or spreading, narrowed into a stalk-like base which is inserted into a raised part of the twig. 2-3.5 cm long, hairless, soft, with a rounded or pointed tip; green above, with 2 white bands beneath.

Flowers: Male flowers yellow, cylindrical and growing beneath the twigs. Female flowers in upright cones, 2-6 cm long, green or red.

Cones: Drooping, 5-10 cm long, light brown and falling off entire. The 3-pointed tips of the bracts are clearly visible.

Bark: At first grey, thin and smooth with resin glands; later becoming red to grey-brown, deeply furrowed, thick and soft (photo p. 246).

Distribution: Pacific North America. Grown in parks in Europe, and one of the most important exotic conifers in the forestry industry..

Habitat: Prefers deep, somewhat acid, light sandy loam soils; not suitable for calcareous soil. A semi-shade species sensitive to late frost.

Note: The natural range of Douglas Fir is very large and covers very different climates. Within this area 2 climatic races are recognized: Green or Coastal Douglas Fir (var. *menziesii*) is found in the very rainy coastal region. This form is best suited for W, C and E Europe. Blue, Mountain or Inland Douglas Fir (var. *glauca*) is found in the mountains and has shorter, blue-green needles and cones 5-6 cm long.

Branch

Shoot: above (l); below (r)

♂ flowers

Characteristic features of Douglas Fir: spindle-shaped buds (l); bracts extending from cone (r)

Eastern Hemlock 🌸☞
Canadian Hemlock
Tsuga canadensis

(Pine Family)

Shape: Tall conifer with a broadly conical crown, growing to about 50 m in its native region and to about 20 m in Europe. The tips of the horizontal branches curve downwards.

Needles: Short-stalked, spreading flat to either side of the shoot; the short needles on the upper side are often twisted, showing pale undersides. 8-18 mm long, flat, gradually narrowing towards the tip, dark green above, white stripes below, surrounded by an obviously greener margin.

Flowers: Male flowers small and cone-shaped. 3-4 mm, yellow-green. Female flowers in upright small cones 5-7 mm long and pale green.

Cones: Usually numerous, drooping and short-stalked, small (1.5-2 cm long) oval and brown. Cones fall off the tree in one piece, but long after the seeds have been shed.

Bark: Grey-brown, with pale furrows (photo p. 246).

Distribution: N E North America. Grown as an ornamental tree in Europe.

Habitat: Shady damp sites (600-1600 m), usually on acid soils. Hardy, drought-sensitive, shallow-rooted shade tree.

Similar species: Western Hemlock.

Eastern Hemlock: underside of twig showing stalked needles (l) unopen ♂ flowers (r)

Small short-stalked cones of Eastern Hemlock

Western Hemlock 🌸

(Pine Family)   *Tsuga heterophylla*

Western Hemlock differs from Eastern (Canadian) Hemlock in the following ways:

Shape: To about 80 m in native range, to about 40 m in Europe. Crown at first conical, later irregularly broad.

Needles: About the same width at the base and tip; on lower surface with a less clear green margin surrounding the 2 pale stripes.

Cones: Unstalked, 2-2.5 cm long (photo p. 246).

Distribution: N W North America. In Europe generally rarer than Eastern Hemlock. Occasionally grown as a forestry tree, particularly in Scotland..

Habitat: Moist sites near the coast.

Similar species: Eastern Hemlock.

Norway Spruce ✣

Picea abies

(Pine Family)

Shape: Upright conifer to 50 m tall with a pointed, conical crown and branches growing in whorls.

Shoot: Hairless or sparsely hairy.

Needles: As in all spruces, the needles grow from small brown pegs: stalk-like extensions of the stem. Radially inserted, spreading only on twigs growing under shade. 1-2.5 cm long. Rectangular, stiff and pointed, dark green along sides. Needles last for 5-7 years.

Flowers: Male flowers found over the entire crown of tree, 1.5-3 cm long, cylindrical, at first red, becoming yellow. Female flowers grow only at the very top of the tree; upright, 2-5 cm long, reddish.

Cones: Drooping, 10-15 cm long, brown; falling from the tree entire. Bracts not visible.

Bark: Grey or red-brown, flaky (photo p. 246).

Distribution: Much of Europe and Asia.

Habitat: Forms woods in Europe in cool, damp mountain sites above 800 m (montane and sub-alpine zone), in the Alps to about 2000 m. Also very widely planted outside this region as a forestry tree. No special soil or climate requirements, but needs a good supply of soil moisture as it is shallow-rooted. Prefers moist, deep, loose loamy soils. Partial shade tree.

Similar species: Oriental Spruce (p. 24), Sitka Spruce (p. 24).

Note: Norway Spruce, the most important European forestry tree, has suffered much in recent years from die-back caused by air pollution. The commonest symptom of this illness is a loss of needles, but the precise causes are still not clear. Commonly used as Christmas tree (see also Silver Fir, p. 8). The three photographs opposite show the adaptation of the tree's shape to its environment. At high altitudes Norway Spruce is usually narrow due to heavy snowfall; at lower levels the trees are broadly conical in shape.

Twig: above (l); below (r). Spruce needles have a stalk-like base

Branch with cones

The ♂ flowers (l) are smaller than the upright young ♀ cones

Oriental Spruce ❀ ☞

Picea orientalis

(Pine Family)

Shape: Coniferous tree to 50 m tall, with conical, pointed crown.

Shoot: Finely hairy.

Needles: Dense, radially arranged on the upper side and more or less spreading beneath. Only 5-10 mm long (this species has the shortest needles of all the spruces), markedly rectangular, stiff, shiny dark green.

Cones: Sep-Oct, drooping, 5-9 cm long, first violet, brown when ripe, resinous.

Bark: Thin, brown and scaly.

Distribution: N Turkey, Caucasus. Planted in parks in Europe.

Habitat: Mountains (800-2000 m).

Similar species: Norway Spruce (p. 22).

Oriental Spruce: branch with ♂ flowers. Pale green is new growth, older needles darker

Oriental Spruce: shoot (above & below) with short, strong needles (l); unripe cones (r)

Sitka Spruce ❀

Picea sitchensis

(Pine Family)

Shape: Grows to 90 m where native; in Europe the maximum is about 50 m. Quick-growing conifer with conical crown.

Shoot: Mostly hairless.

Needles: Radial on the upper side, spreading beneath, 1.5-2.5 cm long, flat, narrow, stiff and sharply-pointed. Shiny green above, silver-grey beneath.

Cones: Aug-Sep, Pale brown, 5-10 cm long, hanging and short-stalked.

Bark: Thin, flaky, grey to reddish-brown.

Distribution: W and N America. Grown in parks and gardens in Europe, forestry tree in coastal regions. Very common forestry species in BI.

Habitat: Lowland sites with a rainy climate and high air humidity.

Similar species: Norway Spruce (p. 22), Colorado Spruce (p. 28).

Crown of Sitka Spruce

Sitka needles are shiny dark green above (l) and silver grey beneath; tips sharply pointed (r)

Serbian Spruce ⊛

Picea omorika

(Pine Family)

Shape: Tall, straight-growing conifer, to 35 m tall, with a dense, narrow, pointed conical crown. When growing in the open it develops branches growing well down the trunk.

Branches: Curved upwards towards the tips.

Shoot: Short and thickly hairy.

Needles: Inserted on small, brown pegs – stalk-like portions of the twig. Radially arranged on twig, but in shady conditions needles somewhat spreading beneath. 1-2 cm long, flat, stiff, blunt or slightly pointed. Shiny, dark green above and with 2 white longitudinal bands beneath. Needles last about 10 years.

Flowers: May. Male flowers 1-2 cm long, pale red. Female flowers in upright cones 1.5-2.5 cm long, reddish.

Cones: Sep-Oct, Hanging, 4-6.5 cm long, dark violet at first, ripening to brown, resinous. Bracts not visible. Cones fall off entire.

Bark: Thin, grey-brown, papery in young trees and cracking into square flakes with age (photo p. 246).

Distribution: A very small area in the Tara Mountains of Bosnia. Grown in parks and gardens in Europe and one of the commonest planted conifers.

Habitat: Mixed woods on calcareous soils on steep shady slopes between 800 m and 1500 m. Tolerates a wide range of soil types and insensitive to water-logging, drought, frost and pollution. Semi-shade species, shallow-rooted.

Note: This species was first discovered in 1887 in its somewhat inaccessible natural habitat.

The photograph opposite shows trees with typically narrow conical crowns.

Shoot: upper side (l) and lower side (r). The needles are flat with 2 white bands beneath

Crown region with cones

Cones (l); ripe open cone (r)

Colorado Spruce ✿

(Pine Family)

Picea pungens

Shape: Rather a bushy conifer growing to 40 m in its natural habitat and to about 25 m in Europe. Dense, broadly conical crown with horizontal branches and twigs.

Shoot: Hairless.

Needles: Radially inserted on short, stalk-like brown portions of the stem. 1.5-3 cm long, mostly slightly curved, rectangular, very stiff and sharply pointed. Needles last from 5-8 years. Variable in colour. The type species is a dull green but there are also blue-green varieties (for example *P. pungens* var. *glauca*).

Flowers: May, male flowers 1-2 cm long, yellow. Female flowers in erect reddish cones, only at the top of the crown.

Cones: Sep-Oct, hanging, unstalked, 7-11 cm long, pale brown and resinous. Falling off entire. Bracts not visible.

Bark: Thick, furrowed, and roughly scaly.

Distribution: C North America. Commonly planted in parks and gardens in Europe.

Habitat: Mixed forest tree found in mountains (1800-3300 m) mainly alongside fast-flowing rivers. Tolerates a wide range of soil types. Not sensitive to frost or air pollution. Needs much space in order to develop its full crown. Shallow-rooted.

Similar species: Sitka Spruce (p. 24).

Note: The green-needled form is much rarer than the decorative glaucous variety (latter often called Blue Spruce).

The photograph opposite shows an older specimen which has branches right down the trunk.

Young Colorado Spruce showing stiff horizontal branches

Twig: the blue-green form is commonly planted

The stiff, pointed needles are mostly curved (l); cones (r)

Wellingtonia 😊 ☞ *Sequoiadendron giganteum*
(Swamp Cypress Family)

Shape: Massive-trunked conifer growing to 85 m in its natural habitat and to about 50 m in Europe. Crown conical.

Needles: Scaly and pointed. Arranged spirally around the twig, 4-7(12) mm long, bluish green. Smell of aniseed when crushed.

Flowers: Apr-May, male flowers small and yellow. Female flowers in small, green cones about 1 cm long.

Cones: Oval, 4-7 cm, at first green, but turning reddish brown and woody in the second year as the seeds ripen.

Bark: Soft, thick, reddish brown and furrowed (photo p. 246). Specimens in parks and gardens often have a ring of paler bark where people have punched the bark to feel its texture.

Distribution: California. Commonly grown in parks and gardens in Europe.

Habitat: Mountain sites (1400-2000 m) with snowy winters and dry summers. Mainly on deep, fertile soils. In Europe somewhat frost-sensitive, but hardy in BI.

Note: Wellingtonias in the Sequoia and Yosemite National Parks in California have been estimated at 2500-3000 years old and may each contain up to 1600 cubic metres of wood.

Wellingtonia: twig, showing tiny pointed needles

Wellingtonia: unripe, green cones

Japanese Red Cedar 😊
(Swamp Cypress Family) *Cryptomeria japonica*

Shape: Conifer growing to 50 m in native sites, in Europe to about 20 m.

Needles: Thin and tapering, arranged spirally along the stem, 0.6-2(3) cm long, curved and pointed, dark green, often brownish in winter.

Cones: Oct, 1.5-3 cm across, brown and rounded. Bracts with thorny appendages.

Bark: Reddish-brown, fibrous and peeling away in strips with age (photo p. 246).

Distribution: Japan. Grown as a decorative tree in Europe. Commoner in the W in BI.

Habitat: Rainy mountain sites (500-1200 m), on moist to damp soils; hardy.

Japanese Cedar: stiff, curved needles (l); rounded cones at end of twig (r)

Swamp Cypress 🌣☞

(Swamp Cypress Family)

Taxodium distichum

Shape: Deciduous conifer growing to 50 m tall.

Shoot: Brownish twigs with long, green deciduous shoots arranged alternately, each shoot 5-15 cm long. *Buds:* Small, rounded.

Needles: 1-2 cm long, flat, soft and pale green (brown in autumn). Alternate, spreading to either side of deciduous shoots. In the autumn the entire shoot falls away with the needles. The woody shoots also have spirally arranged scale leaves.

Flowers: Mar-Apr, male flowers in inflorescences 7-13 cm long. Female flowers in green cones.

Cones: Oct-Nov, rounded, 2-2.5 cm across and brown.

Bark: Grey to reddish-brown with fine longitudinal furrows, becoming soft and stringy later (photo p. 246).

Distribution: S E North America. Parks and gardens in Europe. In BI mainly in S England.

Habitat: Swamps, river valleys, on moist or damp soils. Frost-sensitive when young.

Similar species: Dawn Redwood (p. 34).

Note: Develops knee-like bumps (pneumatophores) from the roots of older trees, particularly when these are growing in swampy conditions or close to water.

Cones of Swamp Cypress (note pale green deciduous shoots)

Swamp Cypress 'knee'

Coast Redwood 🌣

(Swamp Cypress Family)

Sequoia sempervirens

Shape: Conifer. Tallest tree in the world, growing to 110 m in its native region (the record is held by a specimen known as Howard Libby, which has been measured at 112.4 m). In Europe grows to about 40 m.

Needles: Scale-like and spirally arranged on main branches, 3-8 mm long. Needle-shaped on twigs, 6-20 mm long, parted, flat, dark green above, grey-green beneath.

Cones: Oct, Oval, 2-2.5 cm long.

Bark: Thick, soft and reddish brown.

Distribution: Pacific coast of North America. Hardy only in the milder parts of Europe.

Coast Redwood: twig (l); cones (r)

Dawn Redwood ✿

Metasequoia glyptostroboides

(Swamp Cypress Family)

Shape: Rapidly-growing deciduous conifer to 35 m tall, with a conical crown. Trunk shows characteristic pits below the points of insertion of the branches.

Shoot: Brownish long twigs carry opposite, green, deciduous shoots, each 5-15 cm long. *Buds:* Narrowly oval, to 4 mm long, opposite, inserted at an acute or right angle.

Needles: Spirally arranged on the woody twigs, opposite on the short deciduous twigs. Each needle is 1-3.5 cm long, pale green, flat and soft, turning reddish in the autumn. Deciduous twigs fall away with their needles..

Flowers: May, male flowers small and rounded, growing in inflorescences up to 10 cm long. Female flowers in terminal green cones.

Cones: Oct-Dec, oval, with rounded top, long-stalked, 1.5-2.5 cm across, green and upright at first, hanging and brown when ripe.

Bark: Grey to reddish-brown, with longitudinal furrows, becoming soft and stringy with age.

Distribution: N W Hupeh Province in China. Common park and garden tree in Europe. In BI mainly in S.

Habitat: Deep, moist to wet, rich soils. Hardy, but sensitive to late frosts. Semi-shade species.

Similar species: Swamp Cypress (p. 32).

Note: The Dawn Redwood was not discovered alive until 1941, after the genus *Metasequoia* had been described from fossils by a Japanese in the same year. Seeds were then introduced into Europe in 1947, and the tree rapidly spread from that time via cuttings.

Side shoot, with comb of opposite, spreading needles (l); pitted trunk (r)

Branch in autumn: the needles turn red before falling off with the deciduous side shoots

The green unripe cones grow upright; when ripe they hang down

Common Juniper *⊛

(Cypress Family)

Juniperus communis

Shape: Shrub or small coniferous tree growing to 10 m tall, with rather shaggy growth. Very variable in shape, from conical or thin and towering to low-growing or thickly bushy. Branches grow upwards at an acute angle.

Needles: Inserted in whorls of 3, 1-1.8 cm long, stiff and sharply pointed. Hollow on the upper side with a broad greyish-white band, more or less ridged below and green. Needles last for 3-4 years.

Flowers: Male and female flowers on separate plants growing in the axils of the young needles. Male flowers oval, 4-5 mm long and yellow. Female flowers only about 2 mm across, growing in small green cones.

Fruit: Sep-Oct, a fleshy rounded berry-like cone, 5-9 mm across, green at first, ripening (in the second or third year) to blue-black. Botanically Juniper berries are false fruits, being formed from three fused scale-leaves from the female inflorescence.

Bark: Grey or reddish-brown, with longitudinal cracks, peeling

Distribution: Europe, much of Asia, N Africa, North America.

Habitat: From the lowlands right up into the mountains (Alps to 1900 m). Open pinewoods, sunny rocky sites, heaths and poor grassland. Found on a wide range of soil types. Deep-rooted.

Note: Juniper is very variable and may be creeping, bushy or form a tall, narrow tree. The berry-like cones are used in cooking and to add flavour to gin. Common Juniper rarely grows as tall as the tree shown in the photograph opposite.

Twig with berry-like cones

The sharp needles are in whorls of three

Ripe berries (cones)

Monkey Puzzle ✿
Chile Pine
Araucaria araucana

(Monkey Puzzle Family)

Shape: Conifer growing to 50 m in its native region and to about 25 m in
Europe. Male trees usually much smaller than female trees. Trunk
straight and usually branched only towards the top. Crown at first conical,
later more umbrella-shaped. Branches layered, and arranged in whorls.

Needles: Oval to lanceolate, 2.5-5 cm long and up to 2 cm wide at the
base, flat, stiff and leathery, dark green and sharply pointed. The needles
cover the stem in dense overlapping spirals, and remain on the tree for
up to 15 years.

Flowers: Jun-Aug, male and female flowers on separate trees. Male
flowers cylindrical, 8-13 cm long, with many spirally inserted stamens.
Female flowers large, rounded and spiny.

Cones: Upright and rounded to broadly oval, 12-20 cm across, with a
thick covering of sharply pointed scales. Green at first, later turning
brown. 2 or 3 years after flowering, the ripe cones fall from the tree.

Seeds: Elongated, 2-4 cm long, brown and edible.

Bark: Grey-brown and wrinkled.

Distribution: Chile, S W Argentina. In Europe grown as an ornamental tree,
particularly in the British Isles and S Europe; rarer in C Europe.

Habitat: Rainy, mountain sites. Hardy only in the mildest climates.
Prefers rich, moist soils and also does well in coastal sites with strong,
salty winds. Sensitive to dry air.

Crown of young tree

Trunk of young tree showing needles
sticking out (l); the shoots have a dense
covering of overlapping needles (r)

Branch

The large, upright cones fall from the tree
when ripe

Yew * ⚘

(Yew Family)

Taxus baccata

Shape: Small evergreen bushy shrub or small tree to 15m tall. Broadly conical, oval or rounded in outline and usually many-trunked. In old specimens the trunks may join together to form a massive, irregularly-furrowed central trunk.

Needles: Grow radially on erect stems and spreading on horizontal stems. 1-3.5 cm long, 2-3 mm wide, flat, soft and finely pointed. Narrowing into a small stalk at the base. Shiny dark green above with a raised central vein, pale green beneath. Needles last 5-10 years.

Flowers: Mar-Apr, male and female flowers on separate trees, and borne in the leaf axils. Male flowers clustered on undersides of twigs, rounded, 3-4 mm across and yellow. Female flowers 1-2 mm across, green and rather bud-like.

Seeds: Sep-Oct, green and oval at first, later dark brown and hard. Surrounded by fleshy cup-shaped aril, 8-10 mm across, green at first, ripening to bright red (yellow in some varieties).

Bark: Thin, red or grey-brown, smooth and flaky (photo p. 246)

Distribution: Europe, N Africa, Caucasus, Turkey.

Habitat: Lowland to montane levels (to 1400 m in the Alps) mainly in oceanic climates (damp, with mild winters). Sometimes found scattered in the understorey of deciduous woods, particularly on open, calcareous soils in gulleys and on steep slopes. Sensitive to winter and late frosts. Shade species, deep-rooting. Popular park and garden tree.

Notes: All parts of Yew contain the poisonous alkaloid taxin, except for the fleshy aril of the fruit (but seed itself poisonous!). Much reduced in its natural habitat, and protected. There is a wide range of cultivated forms of Yew in parks and gardens.

The photograph (opposite, upper) is *Taxus baccata* 'Fastigiata'. Yew has become rare in its natural habitat (opposite, lower).

The ripe seeds are surrounded by the bright red fleshy aril (l); in the cultivated variety *Taxus baccata* 'Lutea' the aril is yellow (r)

Twigs with ripe seeds

♂ flowers (l); the ♀ flowers resemble buds (r)

40

European Larch ✤

Larix decidua

(Pine Family)

Shape: Deciduous conifer growing to 50 m tall. Rapidly growing at first and with a narrowly conical crown, later broadening and flattening. Branches thin and drooping.

Shoot: Main shoots have a yellowish bark.

Needles: Single and spirally arranged on long shoots, clustered in whorls of 30-50 on short side shoots. 1.5-3 cm long, flat, soft and pale green, turning golden yellow in the autumn.

Flowers: Mar-May, before or simultaneous with the first leaves; borne on the side shoots. Male flowers 5-10 mm across, yellow, clustered on the undersides of the twigs. Female flowers in upright, red cones 1-3 cm long.

Cones: Sep-Oct, upright, 3-4 cm long, oval and brown. Scales straight, edges not rolled outwards. Often remain on the tree for years after ripening.

Bark: Thick grey-brown, often flecked reddish-brown, deeply furrowed and scaly (photo p. 246).

Distribution: Alps, also scattered in the Carpathians, Sudeten Mountains and Poland. Much planted in BI.

Habitat: The main habitat in the Alps is close to the tree line (up to 2400 m), where it forms communities with Arolla Pine. Here the climate is very continental, with harsh winters, short, bright summers and dry air. Also found in the northern Alpine foothills, in mixed stands with Spruce, Fir and Beech. Widely planted by foresters in hilly and lowland sites outside the natural range. Grows on calcareous and acid soils. A light-loving, deep-rooting species.

Similar species: Japanese Larch (p. 44).

The photographs opposite show a group of European Larch in spring (above) and autumn (below).

Branch in autumn; such thin, drooping branches are typical of European Larch

Flowering ♀ cones

Cones: upright scales (l); side shoot, showing needles in clusters

Japanese Larch ✤
(Pine Family)

Larix kaempferi

Shape: Deciduous conifer to 45 m tall. Grows even faster than European Larch when young. Crown broadly conical with horizontal branches turning upwards towards their tips. Branches spread more or less horizontally, not drooping.

Shoot: Long shoots have reddish-brown bark.

Needles: Single, and spirally arranged on long shoots, in whorls of 40-60 on short shoots. 2-3.5 cm long, flat, soft and grey or bluish-green.

Leaves: Turning golden yellow in the autumn.

Flowers: See European Larch (p. 42).

Cones: See European Larch, but somewhat smaller, and with scales turned outwards.

Bark: Red-brown and scaly (photo p. 246).

Distribution: C Japan. In Europe introduced as an ornamental tree. Much planted in BI, also as forestry species.

Habitat: Restricted in the wild to volcanic mountains (1300-2000 m) with rainy summers. In Europe mainly planted in oceanic areas. Wide soil tolerance, but requires a high soil and air humidity, especially in the growing season. Drought-sensitive.

Similar species: European Larch (p. 42).

Note: The Hybrid Larch (*L.* x *marschlinsii* = *L.* x *eurolepis*) is the product of crossing this species with European Larch. This hybrid is useful in forestry because it is very fast-growing. It shows characters intermediate between the two parents.

Branch in autumn, showing more erect twigs, typical of Japanese Larch

Cones are typically clustered; this shows previous year's cones, at flowering time

Cones, showing out-turned scales

Upright ♀ flowers, with ♂ flowers below twig (right of photo)

Atlas Cedar ✿
Atlantic Cedar
Algerian Cedar

Cedrus atlantica

(Pine Family)

Shape: In its native region this coniferous tree grows to 50 m tall, but in Europe rarely gets above 30 m. Crown open at first and broadly conical, later becoming irregular. Top of tree always upright and branches angled upwards..

Needles: Single on long shoots, whorled on short side shoots. These side shoots have up to 3 whorls each with 25-30 needles, representing successive years. 1.5-2.5(3) cm long (on average shorter than those of Cedar of Lebanon) stiff, pointed and green. The garden form 'Glauca' has blue-green to silver-grey needles.

Flowers: Sep-Oct, upright on older side shoots. Male flowers solitary, cylindrical, 3-6 cm long, yellowish or pale pink. Female flowers in small cones about 1 cm long, pale green or reddish. Often flowers in Europe; like all cedars the flowering season is in the autumn.

Cones: Upright, 5-8 cm long, 3.5-4.5 cm across, barrel-shaped or nearly cylindrical and either pointed, flattened or concave at the tip, pale brown and resinous. Seeds ripen in 2nd or 3rd year, and, like those of all cedars, the cones break up while still on the tree.

Bark: Finely furrowed, grey-brown (photo p. 246).

Distribution: Atlas Mountains of Algeria. Often grown in parks in Europe. In BI often in churchyards.

Habitat: Mountain sites (1500-2500 m) with warm, dry summers and snowy winters, usually on calcareous, rich soils. The natural forests have now been reduced to small patches. Although not fully hardy, this species is the least frost-sensitive of the cedars in Europe. Also tolerates drought; requires strong sunlight. The most commonly grown form is the blue-needled 'Glauca' variety.

Similar species: Cedar of Lebanon, Deodar (p. 48).

Compared to large, upright ♂ flowers (l), a ♀ flower (r) is rather small. Cedars flower in autumn

Shoot (l); cone (r)

Branch with upright, barrel-shaped cones

Cedar of Lebanon 🌸 ☞

Cedrus libani

(Pine Family)

Shape: Conifer growing to 40 m tall. Crown at first broadly conical, becoming umbrella-shaped and flattened with strong side branches. These branches grow upwards at first but later on spread out horizontally to give a characteristic layered appearance. The leading shoot of the crown may either be upright or sharply curved to one side.

Needles: Singly and spirally arranged on long shoots, clustered in dense whorls on the side shoots, 1.5-3.5 cm long, stiff and pointed, dark green.

Flowers: Like those of Atlas Cedar.

Cones: Upright, 7-11 cm long, 4-6 cm wide, barrel-shaped. Top flattened or concave, brown.

Bark: Dark grey with fine cracks (photo p. 247).

Distribution: Lebanon, Syria, Turkey. Grown in parks and gardens in Europe. In BI often in churchyards.

Habitat: Mountain sites (1000-2100 m), mostly on calcareous soils. Hardy in the milder parts of Europe.

Similar species: Atlas Cedar (p. 46), Deodar.

Stem showing needles thickly clustered on side-shoots; above (l), below (r)

Cones of Cedar of Lebanon; cedar cones disintegrate on the tree

Deodar 🌸 ☞

Cedrus deodara

(Pine family)

Shape: Conifer growing to 60 m tall. Crown conical, leading shoot curving over, branches horizontal, with their tips drooping downwards. Usually narrower than previous 2 species.

Needles: Single, and spirally arranged on long shoots, whorled on short shoots. 2.5-5.5 cm long (longer than those of the other cedars) thin, soft, bendy and pointed, pale green.

Flowers: Like those of Atlas Cedar.

Cones: Upright, 7-11 cm long and 5-6 cm across, barrel-shaped and rounded at the top, bluish at first, turning red-brown later.

Bark: Finely cracked, dark grey-brown (photo p. 247).

Distribution: W Himalaya. Grown in parks and gardens in Europe. In BI often in churchyards.

Habitat: Mountains (1400-3000 m). Only thrives in the milder parts of Europe; more frost-sensitive than Atlas Cedar and Cedar of Lebanon.

Similar species: Atlas Cedar (p. 46), Cedar of Lebanon.

Scots Pine *⊛

Pinus sylvestris

(Pine Family)

Shape: Conifer growing to 40 m tall. Crown at first conical with branches in whorls, later spreading. Lowland trees have rounded, irregular crowns with large branches; mountain trees tend to be narrower, thinner-branched and pointed.

Needles: In pairs on short shoots, 3-7 cm long, stiff, pointed and blue to bluish-green, sometimes yellow or dark green. Needles last from 3-6 years.

Flowers: May-Jun, male flowers clustered at the base of young shoots, cylindrical, 5-8mm long and yellow. Female cones erect, solitary or in pairs (rarely in fours), terminal, about 5mm long and dark red or violet.

Cones: Short-stalked, oval, 3-7 cm long, grey-brown. Scales usually without an obvious spine. Seeds ripen in the autumn of the cones' second year and are shed in the following spring, after which the cones fall off the tree entire.

Bark: Reddish-brown in the upper part of the trunk and flaky; lower down the trunk thick, grey or brown, roughly furrowed and cracking into plates (photo p. 247).

Distribution: C Northern Europe, Turkey and Siberia. In BI native to Scotland; widely planted.

Habitat: Mainly in lowlands, but in mountains to over 2000 m. Tolerates a range of soils; hardy, not sensitive to drought. In Europe its natural habitat is in the more extreme sites (for example those on very dry, poor sandy, sometimes boggy soils). Widely planted throughout. Semi-shade or light-loving species; deep-rooting.

The ♂ flowers are clustered at the base of the young shoots

Open cones after the seeds have fallen out

Reddish bark towards top of tree

The needles are stiff, pointed and mostly distinctly twisted

Monterey Pine ✿

Pinus radiata

(Pine Family)

Shape: A broadly conical conifer, growing to about 40 m tall.

Shoot: Reddish-brown, hairless.

Buds: Sticky.

Needles: In clusters of 3, long and narrow, to 15 cm, bright green.

Flowers: Mar-May, male flowers yellow-brown, in dense clusters; female flowers reddish-purple, clustered on separate shoots.

Cones: Short-stalked, oval or conical, about 7-14 cm long and with asymmetrical base. At first green, ripening to brown, and remaining on tree for up to several years.

Bark: Dark grey, deeply fissured into parallel ridges.

Distribution: California. Planted for timber, mainly in Britain and France. Occasional in parks and gardens. Commonly planted in W Wales, SW England and Channel Isles, especially near the sea. Self-sown in Cornwall.

Habitat: Dry slopes near the coast.

Similar species: Western Yellow Pine, Jeffrey's Pine (both p. 60).

The photograph opposite shows a young tree in a garden.

Shoot with ♂ flowers

Bark (l), cone: note asymmetrical base (r)

Austrian Pine ✿

Pinus nigra

(Pine Family)

Shape: Conifer growing to 40 m tall. Grows fast when young. Crown conical with whorled branches first, later developing strong horizontal branches.

Buds: 1-2 cm long, pointed and resinous.

Needles: Paired on shoot, 8-16 cm long, stiff, sharply pointed and dark green. Needles lasting 4-7 years.

Flowers: May-Jun, like those of Scots Pine (p. 50) but male flowers larger (2-2.7 cm long). Female cones 0.8-1.2 cm long.

Cones: Short-stalked or unstalked, growing more or less horizontally, oval, 4-9 cm long, pale brown and somewhat shiny. Cone scales often with short spine. Seeds ripen in autumn of second year. In the following spring the cone scales open wide to release the seeds, after which the cones fall away entire.

Bark: Grey-brown to dark grey, flaky and rough when older (photo p. 247).

Distribution: S Europe, Balkans and Turkey. Common in parks and gardens and also planted widely by foresters.

Habitat: Usually on shallow, chalky soils in regions with warm summers but not too dry a climate. Resistant to drought, winter and late frosts and air pollution. Semi-shade species, deeply rooting.

Similar species: Stone Pine (p. 56), Maritime Pine (p. 58).

Note: Corsican Pine, *Pinus nigra* ssp. *laricio*, native to Corsica, Sicily and S.Italy, differs from the Austrian Pine in having a more regular, columnar crown with short side branches, and slender, more flexible, grey-green needles (12-18 cm long). It is less hardy, but much used in England for forestry on sandy soils and is also widely planted, especially near the sea.

Sharply conical, resinous bud

Twig, showing long needles

Cones after seed release

♂ flowers at the base of fresh, not yet elongated shoot

54

Stone Pine

Pinus pinea

(Pine Family)

Shape: Conifer growing to about 25 m with a dense, broad umbrella-shaped, flattened crown. Branches mostly angled sharply upwards..

Buds: 6-14 mm long, not resinous; scales fringed with white and rolling back at the tip.

Needles: In pairs (rarely in 3s) on short shoots. 10-18 cm long, stiff and sharply pointed, pale to dark green. Needles last for 2-4 years.

Flowers: May-Jun, male flowers grouped at the base of young shoots, cylindrical, 1-1.5 cm long, yellow. Female cones about the same length, terminal, erect, solitary or in groups of up to 3.

Cones: Virtually stalkless, oval, 10-15 cm long to 10 cm wide, shiny brown. Scales domed, not spiny. Seed a dark brown edible nut, up to 2 cm long. Seeds ripen in the autumn and winter of the third year after flowering. The lower scales remain on the twig when the cones fall off.

Bark: Grey to reddish-brown, with dark furrows, forming large plates (photo. p. 247).

Distribution: S Europe, Turkey. Rarely planted in BI, mainly in S England.

Habitat: Requires a climate with mild winters and warm, dry summers. Tolerates poor soils and is not sensitive to drought. A characteristic tree of the Mediterranean region, this species has been widely planted, particularly along streets and in parks and gardens, as far North as the southern Alps. This frost-sensitive species does best in the milder oceanic parts of Europe.

Similar species: Maritime Pine p. 58, Austrian Pine p. 54.

♂ flowers develop in place of needles; after flowering lower part of shoot lacks needles (l). Cones (r): 1st year (above) & 2nd year cones

Unripe cones

Tips of young Stone Pines

Maritime Pine ✽☞

Pinus pinaster

(Pine Family)

Shape: Conifer growing to 30 m tall, with a broad, flattened crown when fully grown.

Buds: 1.5-3.2 cm long, not resinous; scales with white fringes and rolling back at the tip.

Needles: Paired (rarely in 3's) on short shoots. Very long (13-23 cm), stiff and sharply pointed, yellow to dark green. Needles last for up to 4 years.

Cones: In whorls of up to 5, short-stalked, oval and very large (10-18 cm long), shiny brown. Scale carries a short spine. Cones often remain on the tree for many years after ripening.

Bark: Thick, grey or reddish-brown, deeply furrowed and scaly (photo p. 247).

Distribution: W Mediterranean area; planted in much of S Europe (often as a source of resin). In BI mainly in S, planted on sandy soils or near the sea.

Habitat: Undemanding, not sensitive to drought.

Similar species: Austrian Pine (p. 54), Stone Pine (p. 56).

Crown of Maritime Pine, showing typical clusters of old cones

Maritime Pine: flowering twig (l); cone showing spiny scales (r)

Aleppo Pine

Pinus halepensis

(Pine Family)

Shape: Conifer growing to about 20 m tall, with a rather twisted trunk. Crown in well-grown specimens is rather irregular, conical or flattened.

Needles: Paired, on short shoots, 6-10 cm long, thin, flexible and pointed, pale or yellowish green. Needles last for about 3 years.

Cones: In whorls of up to 3 on short, powerful stalks, oval, 6-10 cm long, reddish-brown and shiny; scale lacking spine. Cones often stay for the whole year on the tree after ripening.

Bark: Pale grey and smooth at first, becoming furrowed, flaky and grey to reddish-brown in older trees (photo p. 247).

Distribution: Mediterranean region, particularly near the coast. Very rarely planted in BI, mainly in S.

Habitat: Undemanding, drought insensitive.

Aleppo Pine: branch with cones

Western Yellow Pine ✿☞

(Pine Family)   *Pinus ponderosa*

Shape: In its native region this conifer grows up to 70 m tall, but in
Europe is rarely more than 20 m. Branches often drooping
Shoot: Brownish-green and shiny in first year.
Buds: Resinous.
Needles: In 3s on short shoots. Unusually long (12-26 cm), stiff and
pointed, dark or pale green.
Cones: Elongated to oval, 7-15 cm long, pale brown. Cone scales with
straight or somewhat down-curved spine. The lower scales remain on the
tree after the rest of the cone falls away.
Bark: Furrowed, grey to red-brown, often almost black (photo p. 247).
Distribution: W and N America. In Europe mainly in parks. In BI
frequent in gardens, especially in Scotland; rare in Ireland.
Habitat: Mountains (500-2600 m), undemanding, not sensitive to
drought, hardy.
Similar species: Jeffrey's Pine

Western Yellow Pine has very long needles

The cones of the Western Yellow Pine tend
to grow in clusters

Jeffrey's Pine ✿

(Pine Family)   *Pinus jeffreyi*

Shape: Conifer growing to 60 m in native region, in Europe to about 30 m.
Shoot: Covered with bloom in first year. *Buds:* Not resinous.
Needles: In 3s on short shoots. Unusually long (12-22 cm), stiff, pointed,
blue or grey-green.
Cones: Oval, very big (to 25 cm), pale brown. Cone scales with sharp
down-curved spine.
Bark: Furrowed, reddish-brown to blackish, cracking into plates.
Distribution: SW North America. In
Europe in parks. In BI less common
than Western Yellow Pine; rare in
Ireland.
Habitat: Mountain sites (1500-
3000 m) with warm, dry summers
and cold winters; undemanding, not
sensitive to drought, hardy.
Similar species: Western Yellow Pine

Jeffrey's Pine – note the long needles and
large cones (not yet open in this photograph)

Arolla Pine ✿

Pinus cembra

(Pine Family)

Shape: Conifer growing to 25 m tall with a dense, deep crown, at first narrowly conical, later wide and rounded. Trees in their native habitat are often rather irregular, those in cultivation have much more even growth.

Shoot: Covered with rust-red felty hairs.

Needles: In brush-like groups of 5, on short shoots. 5-8 cm long, rather stiff, dark green, with bluish-white bands on the inside. Last for 3-6 years.

Flowers: Jun-Jul, male flowers grouped at the base of the younger shoots, oval to cylindrical, 1-2 cm long, yellow or red. Female young cones upright, solitary or in clusters of up to 5 at the tips of the fresh growth, violet.

Cones: Upright, oval, 5-8 cm long, violet at first and with a bloomy covering, ripening to brown. Seed scales leathery, not woody. The cones fall off the tree unopened with the seeds inside in spring of the third year.

Seeds: Large (1-1.3 cm), brown, unwinged, rather hard, and edible.

Bark: Grey-brown, ridged and scaly.

Distribution: Alps, Carpathians; a sub-species (ssp. *sibirica*) grows in N Russia and W Siberia. Often planted in larger gardens and parks.

Habitat: Mainly in the central Alps (1700-2400 m, up to 2800 m, forming the tree line). Found in areas with a markedly continental climate (hard winters, short, bright summers, dry air). Found on both calcareous and acid soils. Very hardy, and needing only a short growing season (minimum 70 days). Tolerates partial shade when young.

The photographs opposite show isolated trees (above) and a closed stand (below).

The needles grow in groups of 5

Young cones, just after flowering

Arolla Pine cones are violet at first, ripening to cinnamon brown

Weymouth Pine ✿

Pinus strobus

(Pine Family)

Shape: Rapidly-growing conifer, to 60 m in its native region, to about 25 m in Europe. Crown at first conical, later flattening and broadening, irregular. Branches develop horizontally, and turn upwards towards the top of the tree.

Shoot: Thin at first and softly hairy, later hairless.

Needles: In clusters of 5 on short shoots, 6-12 cm long, soft, thin, pale or blue-green, with white longitudinal bands on the inside. Needles last from 2-3 years.

Flowers: May-June, male flowers at the base of new shoots, 5-8mm, cylindrical and yellow. Female young cones narrow, upright and noticeably stalked, 1.5 cm long, greenish, growing at the ends of the shoots.

Cones: 10-20 cm long, pale brown, narrow, cylindrical, slightly curved, drooping, with a 2 cm long stalk. Cone scales leathery, resinous. Ripening in autumn of the second year, cones fall off the tree sometime after releasing their seeds.

Bark: Smooth at first, often shiny and grey-green, later dark grey-brown, ridged and flaky (photo p. 247).

Distribution: E and N America. Commonly planted as an ornamental tree in Europe and also by foresters. In BI sometimes seen in churchyards and parks, and some plantations in W.

Habitat: Hills and lowlands with a cool moist climate. Prefers deep, fresh soils. Not sensitive to frosts. Semi-shade species.

Similar species: Macedonian Pine (p. 66)

Note: Weymouth Pine suffers from blister-rust fungus disease, caused by *Cronartium ribicola*. This has proved practically impossible to control, and the symptoms include resinous swellings of the trunk and branches. It has killed many older trees. The photograph opposite shows Weymouth Pine with horizontal branches with upturned tips.

Year-old cones, showing obvious stalk

Branches with unripe, green cones

Needles clustered in groups of 5 along twig (l); open cones (r)

Bhutan Pine ✿ ☞
Himalayan Pine

Pinus wallichiana

(Pine Family)

Shape: Conifer growing to 50 m in its natural habitat and to about 25 m in Europe. Loose, broadly-conical crown with horizontal branches.
Shoot: Hairless, with a soft bloom.
Needles: In groups of 5 on short shoots. Unusually long (12-20 cm), soft, thin and drooping, bluish-green, with white stripes on the inside.
Cones: 15-26 cm long, pale brown with a 5 cm stalk, very resinous.
Bark: Grey-brown to dark grey, ridged and flaky (photo p. 247)
Distribution: Himalaya. Grown as an ornamental tree in Europe. In BI common in larger gardens and parks.
Habitat: Mountains (1500-4000 m), prefers deeper soils; hardy. Grows best in bright, open conditions.

Bhutan Pine: branch showing large cones

Bhutan Pine: the long needles droop downwards

Macedonian Pine ✿

Pinus peuce

(Pine Family)

Shape: Conifer growing to 25 m tall, with narrowly conical crown.
Shoot: Thick, hairless.
Needles: In groups of 5 on short shoots, each 7-10 cm long, stiff and green with white bands on the inside.
Cones: Like those of Weymouth Pine, but smaller (8-15 cm long) and with a stalk only about 1 cm long. Grey to dark brown, ridged and flaky.
Distribution: Bulgaria, Albania, Macedonia, N Greece. In parks in Europe. In BI occasional in parks and upland plantations, particularly in W.
Habitat: Mountains (800-2300 m), mainly on silicious soils on shady slopes; more rarely on calcareous soils Hardy semi-shade species.
Similar species: Weymouth Pine (p. 54).

Macedonian Pine: needles in groups of 5 along twig (l); cones exuding resin (r)

Monterey Cypress ❀☞

(Cypress Family)   *Cupressus macrocarpa*

Shape: Conifer, to about 35 m tall. Narrow and with conical crown when young, spreading, often becoming flat-topped with age.

Shoot: Point forwards in dense bunches. Covered in scale-leaves. Crushed foliage lemon-scented.

Leaves: Very small, scale-like, pointed, growing pressed close to shoot. Pale margin and dark tip.

Flowers: May-Jun, male flowers green and yellow, about 3 mm across. Female flowers towards outer end of previous season's growth; bright green and cylindrical, about 6 mm long.

Cones: Rounded, purple-brown, about 3-4 cm long, with pointed scales. Old cones remain on tree for several years.

Bark: Brown, with shallow ridges, turning grey with age.

Distribution: Near Monterey, California (rare in wild). Widely planted in W Europe, especially SW England.

Habitat: Coastal cliff-top forests.

Similar species: Italian Cypress.

Note: There are ornamental varieties, with lighter or golden-yellow foliage.

Italian Cypress ❀☞

(Cypress Family)   *Cupressus sempervirens*

Shape: Conifer to about 30 m tall. Either narrow, column-shaped and pointed, with nearly vertical branches (commonest form), or broad, with more or less horizontal branches. Always densely branched.

Shoot: Surrounding branches on all sides. Rounded or weakly rectangular (never flat).

Leaves: Scale-like and opposite, growing densely and covering shoot. Blunt and oval, dark green.

Flowers: Mar-Apr, male flowers club-shaped, 3-6 mm long, yellow-green at first, later turning brownish. Female flowers inconspicuous, about 4-6 mm, in rounded cones, green, clustered near shoot-tips.

Cones: Mar-May, rounded, 2-4 cm across, with 6-12 protective scales, each with a somewhat pointed projection in the middle. Grey-brown, shiny. Seeds ripen in second year, and open cones remain on tree for some time.

Bark: Thin, grey-brown, with narrow, longitudinal, spiral ridges.

Distribution: E Mediterranean, SW Asia. Now found throughout Mediterranean region, of which it is highly characteristic, and N to S Alps. Occasionally planted in BI (notably in Somerset).

Habitat: Natural habitat is montane forest, especially rocky, open and sunny sites. Tolerates summer droughts, and requires mild winters.

Similar species: Monterey Cypress.

Note: There are 2 different growth-forms. The original type (var. *horizontalis*), with a broad crown, grows wild in the E Mediterranean, but is rarely planted. The column-shaped form (var. *sempervirens*) has long been planted in parks, gardens, along streets and in graveyards.

Lawson's Cypress ✿

(Cypress Family)   *Chamaecyparis lawsoniana*

Shape: Conifer growing to 65 m in natural habitat, and to 30 m in Europe. Crown narrow and conical, with drooping top. Branches also drooping at tips.

Shoot: Flat, with horizontal fan-like branches.

Leaves: Opposite, scale-like, oval, pointed. Smaller leaves have longitudinal oil glands (visible when backlit). Dark green above, paler with white margins beneath. Aromatic scent (reminiscent of parsley).

Flowers: Apr, develop in previous autumn at tips of twigs. Male flowers club-shaped, 4-6 mm long, red when open. Female flowers similar in size, rounded, bluish and rather inconspicuous.

Cones: Sep-Oct, round, 7-10 mm across, brown and woody, with 8 shield-like scales, each with a short central spine.

Bark: Grey-brown and smooth at first, becoming reddish or silvery-brown and flaky, with longitudinal ridges (photo p. 247).

Distribution: Along the Pacific coast of North America. Commonly planted in towns and gardens in Britain and Europe; also used as windbreak and in forestry.

Habitat: Moist, coastal hills (to 1500 m). Somewhat drought-sensitive, preferring deeper soils. Hardy. Shallow-rooted shade species.

Similar species: Nootka Cypress (p. 72).

Notes: 1) All *Chamaecyparis* species are poisonous.

2) *Chamaecyparis* is similar to *Thuja*. Distinctive features are the overhanging tip to crown, and round cones. *Thuja* has an upright crown, and more elongated cones.

3) There are many varieties of Lawson's Cypress, of which the 'Glauca' types are particularly popular.

4) In recent years, the fast-growing Leyland Cypress, a garden hybrid of *Cupressus macrocarpa* and *Chamaecyparis nootkatensis*, has been much planted in Britain as a screening hedge round gardens, parks and factories. It resembles species of *Chamaecyparis* but has larger female cones (15-20 mm) and, unlike those of *Chamaecyparis nootkatensis*, the tips of its branches do not droop.

Flowering branch

Underside of shoot (l); rounded cones (r)

Club-shaped ♂ flowers in winter (l); these turn bright red in spring (r)

Nootka Cypress 🌼☞(l)

(Cypress Family)   *Chamaecyparis nootkatensis*

Shape: Conifer to 35 m tall, with a conical crown. Tip of crown and branches drooping.

Shoot: Distinctly rectangular.

Leaves: Opposite, sharply pointed scale-leaves, blue to dark green, with white markings below.

Cones: Sep-Oct, rounded, 1 cm across, grey-brown, the 4 or 6 scales each with a sharp spine, usually ripening in second year.

Bark: Photo p. 247.

Distribution: Along the Pacific coast of North America. Hardy ornamental in Europe. In BI common in parks, gardens and churchyards (and sometimes in forestry), but less so than Lawson's Cypress.

Nootka Cypress: ♂ flowers (l); ♂ flowers and ripening cones (r)

Similar species: Lawson's Cypress (p. 70).

Note: See notes 1 and 2 on p. 70.

Sawara Cypress 🌼☞(r)

(Cypress Family)   *Chamaecyparis pisifera*

Shape: Conifer to 20 m tall.

Leaves: Opposite scale-leaves, with narrow, sharp tips. Foliage dark, shiny green above, speckled white beneath.

Cones: Oct, round, pea-sized.

Distribution: Japan. Hardy ornamental in Europe. In BI common in parks, gardens and churchyards, especially in one of its varieties.

Sawara Cypress: underside of shoot

Note: There are many garden varieties, including 'Squarrosa' with blue or grey-green leaves 5-7 mm long, 'Plumosa' with feathery leaves and 'Filifera' with thread-like drooping shoots. See also notes 1 and 2 on p. 70.

Incense Cedar 🌼☞

(Cypress Family)   *Calocedrus decurrens*

Shape: Conifer to 45 m tall.

Leaves: Scale-leaves in 4s in whorl-like arrangement. Crushed foliage has a smell of shoe-polish.

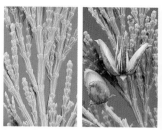

Cones: Sep, oval, 2-2.5 cm long, red-brown, with 6 scales, each with spine at tip.

Distribution: W North America (Oregon, California). Hardy ornamental tree in Europe. Frequent in BI, especially in larger gardens.

Incense Cedar: shoot (l); cones (r)

White Cedar 🪲 ☞
American Arbor-vitae

Thuja occidentalis

(Cypress Family)

Shape: Conifer to 20 m tall, often multi-trunked. Crown conical and upright.

Shoot: Frond-like, flattened, branching horizontally.

Leaves: Opposite, pointed scale-leaves, with conical oil glands, especially on main branches. Dark green above, pale green below without white markings; brownish-green in winter. Aromatic (apple-like, but spicy) scent when crushed.

Flowers: Like those of Western Red Cedar (see p. 76).

Cones: Sep-Oct, oblong, upright, 8-12 mm long, stalked, with 8 or 10 leathery, brown, spreading scales.

Bark: Red-brown to grey-brown, soft, peeling in vertical strips.

Distribution: E North America. Grown in parks, gardens, hedges, graveyards, etc. (more commonly as one of various cultivated varieties).

Habitat: Cool, moist sites, often on wet, calcareous soils. Hardy; shade-species.

Similar species: Chinese Thuja.

Note: Poisonous. See also note 2 on p. 70.

White Cedar: upper surface (l) and lower surface (r) of shoot - note colour difference

White Cedar: the scales spread wide in ripe cones

Chinese Thuja

Thuja orientalis

(Cypress Family)

Shape: Small coniferous shrub or tree (to 12 m), often multi-trunked. Crown conical or rounded, with ascending branches.

Shoot: Frond-like, branching mainly upwards.

Leaves: Like those of White Cedar, but with less obvious and curved oil-glands. Dark green on both sides. Only slight resinous scent when crushed.

Cones: Oct-Nov, rounded oval, 1-2 cm across, brown and woody when ripe. 6 scales, hooked at top, spreading as cone ripens.

Bark: Dull red-brown, peeling in vertical strips. Distribution: E Asia (China). Not commonly planted in BI (mainly midlands).

Note: Poisonous. See also note 2 on p. 70.

Chinese Thuja: young tree showing vertical branching (l); shoot (r)

Western Red Cedar 🏵 ☞

Thuja plicata

(Cypress Family)

Shape: Conifer, growing to 60 m tall in native region, and to about 40 m in Europe. Crown conical and upright.

Shoot: Frond-like, flat and horizontally branching.

Leaves: Opposite scale-leaves, pointed on stronger shoots and with oil-glands, rather blunter on finer shoots, oil-glands inconspicuous or absent; shiny dark green above, grey beneath. Aromatic scent of pineapple, even without crushing.

Flowers: Mar-May, male and female flowers separate on same plant, developing at ends of twigs in previous autumn. Male flowers yellow-brown, rounded, 1-2 mm across. Female flowers in inconspicuous clusters, about 2 mm across.

Cones: Aug-Sep, narrowly oval, 1-1.5 cm long, with 10 or 12 leathery brown, spreading scales.

Bark: Red-brown, soft, peeling into vertical strips (photo p. 247).

Distribution: Pacific coast of North America. Commonly planted in parks, gardens, and as occasional forestry species.

Habitat: Cool, moist sites, often alongside streams. Damp or wet soils, drought-sensitive. Hardy, shallow-rooting shade species.

Note: Poisonous. See also note 2 on p. 70.

Western Red Cedar: shoot has shiny green upper surface (l), grey-green lower surface (r)

Western Red Cedar: unripe cones (l)
Hiba: cones (r)

Hiba 🏵

Thujopsis dolabrata

(Cypress Family)

Hardy Japanese conifer, commonly planted in large gardens, especially in W of BI. Small tree or shrub. Differs from *Thuja* in its broader, hard, leathery scale-leaves; shiny green above, and with characteristic bright white markings beneath with clear green border. Cones rounded. Bark red-brown (photo p. 247).

Hiba: bright white markings on underside of shoot

Walnut ✿

(Walnut Family)

Juglans regia

Shape: Deciduous tree growing to 25 m tall with a broad trunk, loose, open crown and heavy branches.

Shoot: Hairless.

Leaves: Alternate, pinnate, 20-45 cm long with 5-9 (usually 7) elliptical leaflets and a somewhat larger terminal leaflet.

Leaflets: Each about 6-15 cm long, hairless, with entire margins. Terminal leaflet somewhat larger and stalked. Aromatic when bruised.

Flowers: May, opening shortly before the leaves, Male flowers in drooping catkins at the end of the previous year's growth, each 6-13 cm long and yellowish-green. Female flowers in groups of 1-5 on current year's growth, each with 2 large red or whitish crumpled stigmas.

Fruit: Sep-Oct, a single-seeded round to oval fruit, 4-5 cm across. The outer husk is shiny and green at first, ripening to brown. This encloses a hard, woody nut which in turn contains the familiar edible walnut.

Bark: Deeply fissured, dark grey (photo p. 248).

Distribution: Originally SE Europe, SW and C Asia. Intensively cultivated in S and W central Europe and occasionally naturalized. In BI commonly planted, especially in S and SW.

Habitat: From lowlands up to montane levels (rarely above 800 m) in areas with a mild climate (characteristic of wine growing regions). Naturalized in mixed river-valley woodland (for example along the Rhine and Danube rivers). Prefers deep, calcareous soils; sensitive to winter and late frosts, deep-rooted; light-loving species.

Walnut comes into leaf rather late (late April to mid-May), see photograph opposite (above); the lower picture shows Walnut in summer.

Fruits

Shoot with young fruits; the leaves are often slightly pink on first opening

♂ catkins (l); ♀ flowers, showing large, crumpled stigmas (r)

Black Walnut ☞

Juglans nigra

(Walnut Family)

Shape: Deciduous tree to 50 m tall.

Shoot: With short hairs.

Leaves: Large, 25-60 cm long, pinnate, with 11-23 narrowly elliptical, pointed leaflets, each 5-12 cm long and finely-toothed, terminal leaflet smaller. Leaf-stalk hairy.

Fruit: Sep-Oct, rounded, 4-5 cm across, with a thick, rough green aromatic husk. Inside is the black hard nut containing the seed.

Bark: Dark brown, deeply furrowed (photo p. 248).

Distribution: E North America. Grown in parks in Europe. Rarely planted in BI, mainly in S and E England.

Habitat: Deep, rich soils. Hardy, but sensitive to late and early frosts. Light-loving species.

Black Walnut: leaf

Black Walnut: fruits

Shagbark Hickory

Carya ovata

(Walnut Family)

Shape: Deciduous tree to 35 m tall.

Leaves: Pinnate, to 35 cm long, with 5 elliptical leaflets, each up to 17 cm long, the 3 terminal leaflets noticeably larger than the lower pair. Leaflets finely-toothed.

Flowers: Male catkins in stalked groups of 3.

Fruit: Sep, 4-6 cm across, rounded. The green husk has 4 grooves and encloses a pale, shelled, sweet, white edible nut.

Bark: Flaking off in strips.

Distribution: E and N America. Grown in parks in Europe. Uncommon in BI, mainly in S and W.

Habitat: Rich, moist soils.

Shagbark Hickory: leaf (l); fruits, showing grooved husk (r)

Tree of Heaven ✿☞

Ailanthus altissima

(Tree of Heaven Family)

Shape: Rapidly-growing deciduous tree to 25 m tall.

Leaves: Large, 40-60(90) cm long, pinnate, with 13-25(41) narrowly elliptical leaflets. Leaflets reach 7-12 cm long and have large, gland-bearing teeth towards base.

Flowers: Jun-Jul, hermaphrodite or unisexual, often male and female flowers on separate plants. Small, greenish-white, in upright panicles to 25 cm long.

Fruit: Sep-Oct, densely clustered, each 3-5 cm long, with thin, papery wing.

Bark: Smooth, with pale longitudinal stripes (photo p. 248).

Distribution: China. A common decorative tree in the warmer parts of Europe, often naturalized. In BI mainly in SE England

Habitat: Requires strong light and warm conditions, otherwise wide tolerance.

Tree of Heaven: leaves - the leaflets have large teeth towards the base

Tree of Heaven: clustered, winged fruits

Caucasian Wingnut ✿

Pterocarya fraxinifolia

(Walnut Family)

Shape: Deciduous tree to 20 m tall, with domed crown.

Leaves: 20-40(60) cm long, pinnate, with 11-25 narrowly elliptical leaflets. Leaflets each 6-12 cm long and toothed. Leafstalk hairless.

Flowers: Apr-May, male catkins 6-14 cm long, yellow; female catkins up to 20 cm long and greenish.

Fruit: Oct, In long, drooping clusters, 30-60 cm. Each fruit is a small, pale green nutlet, 1.5-2.5 cm across, surrounded by 2 semi-circular wings.

Bark: Dark grey with longitudinal furrows (photo p. 248).

Distribution: Caucasus, NW Iran. Decorative tree in Europe. Occasionally planted in BI.

Habitat: Prefers moist or damp soils close to water; hardy.

Caucasian Wingnut often has several trunks

Caucasian Wingnut: shoot with dangling clusters of fruits

Rowan *⊛
Mountain Ash

Sorbus aucuparia

(Rose Family)

Shape: Fast-growing deciduous tree to 15(20) m; loose, rounded crown, often multi-stemmed.

Buds: Dark violet, not sticky, covered with white, felty hairs

Leaves: Alternate, pinnate, 10-20 cm long, with 9-17 narrowly elliptical, pointed leaflets, each 2-6 cm long and coarsely toothed. Grey-green below, hairy or smooth; dark red or yellow in autumn.

Flowers: May-Jun, hermaphrodite, to about 1 cm across, with 5 white petals, normally 3-styled. Borne in large clusters to about 15 cm across. Flowers have a rather unpleasant smell.

Fruit: Aug-Oct, in dense bunches. Each is a small, rounded, apple-like fruit (pome) usually containing 3 seeds. Yellow, later turning orange-red. Fruits remain on tree until well into winter.

Bark: Smooth, shiny grey, with long, horizontal lenticels (photo p. 148). Older trees sometimes develop dark grey ridged bark towards the base.

Distribution: Europe, W Siberia, Turkey.

Habitat: Found growing at all levels, in the mountains right up to the tree-line (inner Alps up to 2400 m). Found in deciduous and coniferous woodland, woodland clearings and margins; also in scrub and alongside footpaths. An undemanding pioneer species, doing well even on fairly poor, dry acid soils. Grows best however on moist, humus-rich sites. Not sensitive to frost; fairly deep-rooted species, adapted to growing in strong light or in semi-shade. Commonly planted as a decorative tree.

Similar species: True Service Tree (p. 86).

Leaf, showing sharply toothed leaflets

Fruits

Shoot

White flowers, in dense clusters (compound corymbs)

Hupeh Rowan ✿ ☞

Sorbus hupehensis

(Rose Family)

Shape: Deciduous tree growing to about 12 m tall.

Leaves: Pinnate, with up to 17 leaflets, and to about 15 cm long, rather silvery grey-green. Each leaflet is about 6 cm x 2 cm, and is toothed only towards the tip. Green-blue above, grey-blue beneath, turning red in autumn.

Flowers: April-May, in loose, rounded clusters. Each flower is white, with 5 petals and about 6 mm across.

Fruit: Sep-Oct, clusters of small, rounded berries, each about 8 mm across. White, flushed pink towards top.

Bark: Grey, smooth.

Distribution: China. Commonly planted in parks and gardens.

Habitat: Mountain woods.

Similar species: True Service Tree°, *S. domestica*, has pinnate leaves, to 22 cm long, with up to 21 long, toothed leaflets. Its white flowers grow in rounded clusters, and the relatively large fruits are yellow-green (red in one variety). This is a rare tree in the British Isles, recently re-discovered in S Wales. It is scattered in the wild, mainly in S and E Europe and SW Asia, and is not often planted.

Note: Several related Asiatic species with pinnate leaves are increasingly grown in gardens in the British Isles. One of the commonest is Hupeh Rowan, *Sorbus hupehensis* (above).

Kashmir Rowan, *S. cashmiriana*, is another, a native of W Himalaya. It is sometimes planted in parks and gardens, and is best known for its large, white berries. Like the other species on this page, it has pinnate leaves.

Hupeh Rowan: leaf and fruits

True Service Tree: leaf

Common Laburnum 🌼☞

(Pea Family)

Laburnum anagyroides

Shape: Deciduous tree or shrub growing to about 9 m tall.

Leaves: Alternate (may be whorled on short shoots), long-stalked, trifoliate. Leaflets elliptic, 3-6 cm long with entire margins; pale to grey-green beneath, with silky hairs.

Flowers: May-Jun, yellow pea-like flowers in drooping racemes 10-20 cm long.

Fruit: Aug-Sep, pale brown pods 4-8 cm long, silkily hairy at first, later hairless.

Bark: Smooth greenish-brown (photo p. 248).

Distribution: SE Europe, S Alps, S France. Commonly planted as a decorative tree or shrub and sometimes naturalized.

Habitat: Sunny woodland and scrub (to 2000 m). Dry, rich calcareous soils.

Similar species: Alpine Laburnum 🌼 (*Laburnum alpinum*) has flowers clustered in long, slender racemes (to 45 cm). Mountains of SC Europe. In BI planted, particularly in the N

Note: Both these species contain the poisonous alkaloid cytisin. The seeds are particularly dangerous since they resemble small peas. *Laburnum* x *watereri* is an attractive hybrid between these 2 species and is commonly grown in gardens. It has the large flowers of Common Laburnum and racemes as long or even longer than those of Alpine Laburnum.

Common Laburnum: trifoliate leaves

Silver Wattle 🌼
'Mimosa'

Acacia dealbata

(Pea Family)

Shape: Evergreen, broadleaved tree growing to about 20 m tall, with alternate, twice-pinnate leaves. The 10-18 pairs of leaflets are themselves pinnate and have many 3-4 mm long lobes, covered in silvery hairs.

Flowers: Jan-Apr, in small, compact heads, arranged in loose panicles; bright yellow and fragrant.

Fruit: Reddish-brown pods.

Distribution: SE Australia. Often planted in BI, especially in milder SW, and in S Europe.

Silver Wattle: twice-pinnate leaf (l); compact flowerhead, in loose panicle (r)

Silver Wattle: shoot, showing feathery leaves

False Acacia
Black Locust ✤

Robinia pseudoacacia

(Pea Family)

Shape: Fast-growing deciduous tree to about 25 m. Trunk often twisted; crown open and rounded.

Shoot: Ribbed, with paired thorns.

Leaves: Alternate, 20-30 cm long, pinnate, with 9-19 narrowly elliptic leaflets, each 3-5 cm long, with entire margins. Leafstalk has 2 sharp thorns (specialized stipules) at its base. Comes into leaf rather late.

Flowers: May-June, white, 1.5-2.5 cm, pea-like and fragrant, in dense hanging racemes. The flowers are a very rich source of nectar (a good bee plant).

Fruit: Oct-Nov, 5-11 cm long, brown, leathery pods, each with 4-10 brown seeds. Old pods remain on the tree until the following year.

Bark: Pale grey to grey-brown and deeply-furrowed (photo p. 248).

Distribution: E and C North America. In Europe one of the most widespread exotic tree species, found in woods, parks and gardens. In BI naturalized in S.

Habitat: Warm sites in lowland and hills. Undemanding, found on damp, rich, loamy soils as well as on poor, dry, sandy soils; avoids water-logged conditions. Hardy, but sensitive to early frosts. A pioneer species, often growing on waste land, rapid-rooting; for this reason often planted to help stabilize loose soils. The roots absorb atmospheric nitrogen by means of symbiotic bacteria. The leaves are also a rich source of nitrogen.

Note: Most parts of this species are poisonous.

The photographs opposite are of tree crown, showing characteristic bark on trunk and branches (above) and the tree in flower (below).

Shoot with leaves

Leaves, showing thin leaflets

Dangling clusters (racemes) of flowers (l); flattened, leathery fruit pods (r)

Honey Locust ☞

Gleditsia triacanthos

(Pea Family)

Shape: Deciduous tree to 30 m tall.
Shoot: Older shoots have sharp simple or branched thorns.
Leaves: Alternate, pinnate or twice-pinnate. Pinnate leaves 10-20 cm long, with 16-30 oval leaflets. Leaflets 1.5-3.5 cm long, with a weakly-notched margin. Twice-pinnate leaves to 30 cm with 6-12 pinnate leaflets. Leaves turn golden yellow in autumn.
Flowers: Jun-Jul, individual flowers inconspicuous, with 3-5. petals, arranged in racemes.
Fruit: Oct, dark brown, often spirally twisted pod, 20-40 cm long.
Bark: Grey to blackish, scaly, with bunches of dangerously sharp, simple or branched spines, each up to 20 cm long.
Distribution: C North America. In Europe grown in parks and gardens (usually as the non-spiny variety). In BI uncommon; mainly in some southern English parks and gardens.
Habitat: Damp, calcareous soils; wide tolerance; hardy.

Honey Locust: leaf (l); fruits (r)

Honey Locust: trunk with bunches of spines

Kentucky Coffee Tree

Gymnocladus dioicus

(Pea Family)

Shape: Thorny, deciduous tree to 25 m tall.
Leaves: Twice-pinnate, to 90 cm long; leaflets oval and pointed, 3-7 cm long, with entire margins.
Flowers: May-Jun, tree dioecious. Male trees have panicles. about 3 cm long, females have panicles up to 10 cm long. Flowers are whitish, fragrant, and about 2.5 cm across.
Fruit: Dark brown pods about 10-20 cm long, falling off unopened during the winter.
Distribution: C and N America. Found in parks and gardens as a hardy species. Rather rare in BI; mainly in large gardens in S England and Ireland.

Kentucky Coffee Tree: shoot with twice-pinnate leaves

Golden Rain Tree ✿ ☞

(Lychee Family)   *Koelreuteria paniculata*

Shape: Spreading deciduous tree growing to about 12 m.

Leaves: Alternate, pinnate, to 45 cm long. Leaflets to about 10 cm long, toothed, softly hairy, dark green above, turning yellow in autumn.

Flowers: Jul-Sep, each flower is yellow, with 4 petals and about 1.2 cm across. They are grouped in upright conical panicles to about 45 cm long.

Fruit: Triangular, inflated bladder-like capsules, each to 5 cm long, green, ripening to yellow-brown.

Bark: Pale brown, with shallow fissures.

Distribution: China, Korea. In BI uncommon, mainly in large gardens in S.

Habitat: Hot, dry river valleys.

Golden Rain Tree in flower

Pagoda Tree ✿ ☞

(Pea Family)   *Sophora japonica*

Shape: Spreading, rounded, deciduous tree to 25 m tall.

Shoot: Remains green for several years.

Leaves: Alternate, 15-25 cm long, pinnate, with terminal leaflet. Leaflets 7-15, short-stalked, lanceolate to ovate, each 3-5.5 cm long, pointed, with entire margins, dark green above, grey-green and finely hairy beneath.

Flowers: Jul-Aug, individual flowers 1-2 cm long, creamy-white, in upright panicles.

Fruit: Pods, 5-8 cm long, constricted between seeds (up to 6).

Bark: Grey-brown, ridged.

Distribution: China, Korea. Planted as a hardy, decorative tree in Europe. In BI uncommon; large gardens and parks, mainly in the S.

Habitat: Woods in dry mountain valleys.

Ashleaf Maple ⊗
Box Elder

Acer negundo

(Maple Family)

Shape: Medium-sized, quick-growing deciduous tree to about 20 m tall, often multi-branched, with an open, irregular, broad crown. Tips of branches often drooping.

Shoot: Pea green, with waxy bloom.

Leaves: Opposite, long-stalked, about 15-25 cm long, pinnate, with 3-7 (usually 5) thin, narrowly-oval leaflets. Leaflets 5-10 cm long, pointed, with irregular coarse teeth or, more rarely, with entire margins. Terminal leaflet deeply-lobed or trifoliate.

Flowers: Tree dioecious. Male flowers yellowish, in hanging bunches. Female flowers hanging down in longer tassels.

Fruit: Jul-Aug, pairs of winged, pale yellow fruits. Wings curved inwards at an acute angle. Ripe fruits remain on the tree until winter.

Bark: Grey-brown and narrowly fissured.

Distribution: C and E North America. In Europe commonly planted in parks and gardens and occasionally naturalized.

Habitat: Natural habitat is alongside water on damp soils. Also found away from water as long as soil is not too dry. Hardy and relatively insensitive to air pollution. Light-loving species.

Note: There are many garden varieties of Ashleaf Maple. One of the most popular is 'Variegatum' with white-margined leaflets.

Twig, showing opposite branching. The shoot is often pea green, with a waxy bloom

Shoot

Leaf (l); fruits, showing curved wings (r)

Leaves of variegated variety

Horse Chestnut ✿

Aesculus hippocastanum

(Horse Chestnut Family)

Shape: Deciduous tree growing to about 30 m tall, with a broad, dense crown. Main trunk rather short and twisted.

Buds: Large, shiny, reddish-brown and sticky.

Leaves: Opposite, long-stalked, palmate, with 5-7 long, obovate leaflets radiating from a central point. Leaflets to about 25 cm long, double-toothed at margins, dark green above, paler green below. Turning yellow in the autumn.

Flowers: May-Jun, after the leaves have opened, in large (20-30 cm) upright, many-flowered panicles. Petals 5(4) white with a yellow blotch, which later turns red. Flower usually with 7 long, curved stamens.

Fruit: Sep-Oct, round, to 6 cm across, green, covered with flexible spines. Seeds (1-3) large, shiny, dark brown 'conkers'.

Bark: At first smooth, later grey-brown and scaly (photo p. 248).

Distribution: Balkans, (Albania, N Greece, Bulgaria); introduced elsewhere in Europe and commonly planted. Naturalized in some places.

Habitat: Shady, damp, mountain woodland. Prefers rich, deep, moist, sandy or loamy soils. Hardy, shallow-rooted, semi-shade species.

Similar species: Red Horse Chestnut (*Aesculus* x *carnea*) differs in the following ways: leaflets usually somewhat smaller and darker; often short-stalked. Flowers are red and fruits smaller, often without prickles. Of garden origin.

The photographs opposite show a Horse Chestnut just before leaves have opened (above), and in full flower (below).

Flowers of normal (l) and Red (r) Horse Chestnut

Fruit: normal (l) and Red (r) Horse Chestnut

Horse Chestnut: autumn leaves

Red Horse Chestnut: leaf

Common Ash *⚘

(Ash Family)

Fraxinus excelsior

Shape: Deciduous tree to 30(40) m tall with rounded or oval crown. Has a narrower growth form in closed stands.

Buds: Matt black.

Leaves: Opposite, to 35 cm long, pinnate, with 9-15 leaflets. Leaflets narrowly elliptical and pointed, 4-10 cm long, unstalked (except for terminal leaflets), with finely-toothed margins. Leaves open late and fall while still green in the autumn.

Flowers: Apr-May, before the leaves open, trees may be monoecious or dioecious, and the flowers hermaphrodite or unisexual, arranged in many-flowered panicles, at first upright, but later drooping, at the tips of the previous year's growth. Individual flowers are inconspicuous and lack petals. Stamens 2(3), are brownish-red to violet; ovary has 2-lobed stigma.

Fruit: Aug to Oct, hanging clusters of the familiar Ash 'keys', each 2-4 cm long, ripening from green to brown. Ripe keys stay on the tree for a long time.

Bark: Pale grey and smooth at first, becoming dark and ridged (photo p. 248).

Distribution: Europe, Turkey.

Habitat: Mixed deciduous woods, from lowland to montane levels (Alps to 1300 m). Often grows alongside rivers or small streams in hills. Grows best on moist, deep, rich, calcareous soils, but often found on drier, more shallow soils as well. Commonly planted in parks and along roads. Sensitive to late frosts. Deep-rooted semi-shade species.

Similar species: Manna Ash, Narrow-leaved Ash (p. 102).

The photographs opposite show Common Ash in summer (above) and winter (below).

Leaf, showing unstalked leaflets (l); matt black buds (here a large, terminal bud & two opposite lateral buds in axils of leaf stalks) (r)

The small clusters of flowers appear before the leaves

Shoot

Clustered fruits: unripe (l) and ripe (r)

Manna Ash ☹☞

Fraxinus ornus

(Ash Family)

Shape: Often multi-trunked deciduous tree, growing to 20 m tall.

Buds: Grey-brown, felty.

Leaves: Opposite, to 30 cm long, pinnate, with 7-9 narrowly elliptical, pointed leaflets. Leaflets 4-8 cm long with short, often hairy, stalks and finely-toothed margins.

Flowers: Apr-Jun, appearing with the leaves, hermaphrodite, rarely unisexual. In large, upright or drooping terminal panicles. Petals 4, narrow and white. Flowers strongly-scented

Fruit: Aug-Oct, similar to those of Common Ash, but somewhat smaller (2-3 cm long), dark brown.

Bark: Photo p. 248.

Distribution: S Europe (as far N as the S edge of the Alps), Turkey. Grown elsewhere in Europe as an ornamental tree in parks, gardens and on roadsides.

Habitat: Sub-mediterranean mixed broadleaved woodland and scrub, (often with Hop Hornbeam, Downy Oak and Holm Oak). Sunny, rocky slopes, particularly on calcareous soils. Warmth- and light-loving species.

Similar species: Common Ash (p. 100), Narrow-leaved Ash.

Note: Cultivated in S Italy and Sicily for the sugar or syrup (manna) which exudes from damaged stems.

Manna Ash: grey-brown buds (l); leaf showing short-stalked leaflets (r)

Manna Ash: inflorescence (l) and fruits (r)

Narrow-leaved Ash ☞

Fraxinus angustifolia

(Ash Family)

Differences from Common Ash: Buds dark brown; leaflets mostly lanceolate; flowers and fruits in racemes.

Distribution: S and SE Europe, N Africa, Turkey Occasionally grown in parks in Europe. In BI rather rare, mainly in parks in S England.

Habitat: River valley woods.

Narrow-leaved Ash: shoot

Elder *

Sambucus nigra

(Honeysuckle Family)

Shape: Broad-crowned deciduous shrub or small tree to about 10 m tall, with a rather twisted growth and arching branches.

Shoot: Grey-brown with corky warts (lenticels); pith white.

Leaves: Opposite, to 30 cm long, pinnate with 5(3-7) oval, elliptical, pointed leaflets with toothed margins, each up to 20 cm long. Foliage has rather unpleasant smell. Comes into leaf early (Mar-Apr).

Flowers: May-Jun, in many-flowered terminal panicles. Flowers 5-partite, 6-10 mm across, with white or yellowish-white petals; fragrant.

Fruit: Sep-Oct, berries 5-8 mm across, at first red, ripening to black; edible. Fruit stalks red.

Bark: Grey-brown, with longitudinal furrows (photo p. 248).

Distribution: Most of Europe, W Siberia, Caucasus, Turkey.

Habitat: From lowlands to montane zone (Alps to 1500 m) in woodland clearings, hedgerows and scrub. On moist, humus-rich and fertile deep soils. Often on very nitrogen-rich sites. Shallow-rooting light-loving or semi-shade species.

Similar species: Alpine Elder or Red-berried Elder (*Sambucus racemosa*). Differences from Common Elder: *Shape:* A shrub growing to 4 m. *Shoot:* Pith pale brown. *Leaves:* Narrowly elliptical leaflets. *Flowers:* Yellow-green, in panicles. *Fruit:* Red.

The photographs opposite show that Elder sometimes grows into a tree (above) but Alpine Elder is always a shrub (below).

Elder: ripe fruits

Elder: shoot and leaf

Elder: flowers in panicle

Alpine Elder: rounded panicles (l); bright red fruits (r)

Sycamore ⊛

Acer pseudoplatanus

(Maple Family)

Shape: Deciduous tree to 35 m tall with a strongly branched, domed crown.

Leaves: Opposite, very variable in size. Leaf stalk to 20 cm long, lacking milky juice. Leaf-blade 10-20 cm long and about the same width, with 5 oval, pointed lobes with wedge-shaped separations between. Margin irregularly toothed or notched. Uniformly dark green above, paler beneath and greyish-green, at first hairy but becoming hairless, except for the vein axils. Becoming golden yellow in autumn.

Flowers: May, with the leaves, in drooping, many-flowered panicles, 5-15 cm long. Hermaphrodite or unisexual; 5-partite, yellow-green, petals very short.

Fruit: Sep-Oct, winged, each half about 3-5 cm long and set at an acute angle to each other. Fruit halves separating when ripe.

Bark: At first grey-brown and smooth, later scaly, with reddish markings (photo p. 148).

Distribution: Mountains of C, S and SE Europe, Caucasus. Not native in BI, but one of our commonest trees.

Habitat: Common in montane mixed Beech forest and also in shady mountain valley woods; more rarely in sub-alpine Spruce woods (Alps to 1700 m). Prefers deep, moist or damp, fertile base-rich soils in cool, humid sites. Sensitive to flooding. Fairly deep-rooted semi-shade species. Commonly planted along streets, in parks and gardens and sometimes as a forestry tree. Frequently self-sown.

Similar species: Norway Maple (p. 108), Heldreich's Maple (p. 112).

Note: The tree normally known as Sycamore in North America is a species of plane, *Platanus occidentalis* (p. 208).

The photographs opposite show Sycamore in winter (above) and in spring (below).

Flowers in drooping panicle (l); clustered winged fruits (r)

Branch with leaves

Lobed leaf, with wedge-shaped separations between the lobes

Norway Maple ✿

Acer platanoides

(Maple Family)

Shape: Dense-crowned deciduous tree growing to 25(35) m tall

Leaves: Opposite, very variable in size; leaf-stalk up to 17 cm long, containing milky juice; blade 8-17 cm long and 10-20 cm wide, with 5-7 lobes each with pointed teeth and with round separations between. Leaves somewhat glossy on both sides, pale green and hairless on the underside except for the vein axils. Autumn colouring yellow to gold, sometimes red.

Flowers: Apr-May, before the leaves appear, in upright, many-flowered terminal panicles. Hermaphrodite or unisexual, 5-partite, yellow-green.

Fruit: Sept-Oct, paired winged fruits, each wing about 4-5 cm long, set at a wide angle to each other.

Bark: Pale grey and smooth, becoming dark grey to blackish with vertical furrows; not scaly.

Distribution: Much of Europe, Caucasus, Turkey. Introduced to BI, but often self-sown from plantings.

Habitat: From the lowlands to montane levels (Alps to 1100 m); occasionally in mixed broadleaved woods (Oak-Hornbeam woodland, Oak-Elm river valley woodland, mixed Lime woodland). Prefers moist to damp, rich, loose loamy soils. Fairly deep-rooted semi-shade species. Widely planted in parks, gardens and along streets.

Similar species: Sycamore (p. 106), Sugar Maple (p. 112).

The photographs opposite show tree in flower (above) and a view up into the crown (below).

Lobed leaves, with pointed teeth

Leaf emerging from bud as bud-scales turn back

Erect inflorescence

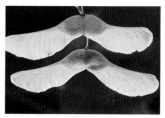

Paired winged fruits, showing wings set at a wide angle or horizontal

Field Maple ✿ 🍂 ☞

(Maple Family)

Acer campestre

Shape: Round-crowned deciduous tree to about 12(20) m tall.

Leaves: Opposite, leaf-stalk with milky juice. Blade 4-8 cm long, 5-10 cm wide, with 5 (rarely 3) blunt lobes, the front 3 lobes often with smaller side lobes towards their tips. Autumn colour yellow or red.

Flowers: Apr-May, appearing with the leaves, in upright or overhanging panicles. Hermaphrodite or unisexual; 5-partite, yellow-green.

Fruit: Aug-Sep, the paired winged fruit has wings set horizontally, not angled.

Bark: Pale brown and smooth at first, developing corky ridges and becoming grey-brown (photo p. 248).

Distribution: Europe, N Africa, Turkey, Caucasus. In BI native in lowland England and Wales.

Habitat: Mixed broadleaved woods in lowland and hills, woodland edges, hedgerows, scrub. Somewhat warmth-loving, preferring dry to moist, rich calcareous soils. Fairly deep-rooted semi-shade species.

Similar species: Montpelier Maple.

Field Maple: twigs often have corky ridges (l); leafy twig (r)

Field Maple: the fruit wings are often reddish

Montpelier Maple

(Maple Family)

Acer monspessulanum

Shape: Tree or shrub to 10 m tall.

Leaves: Opposite, leathery. Stalk lacking milky juice. Blade 3-6 cm long, 4-8 cm wide, with 3 oval lobes with entire margins.

Fruits: Aug-Sep, paired winged fruits, wings set at an acute angle to each other or even parallel.

Distribution: Mediterranean region, SC Europe, from E France to middle Rhine Valley. Rare and not native in BI – mainly a few parks in S England.

Habitat: Warm, mixed broadleaved woods and dry rocks.

Similar species: Field Maple

Montpelier Maple: shoot with leaves (l); fruits showing almost parallel wings (r)

Sugar Maple 🌸 ☞

Acer saccharum

(Maple Family)

Shape: Deciduous tree to about 35 m tall, with a round crown
Leaves: Opposite, 8-15 cm long and about the same width, 5-lobed.
Lobes pointed, with a small number of rather prominent teeth; spaces
between lobes rounded. Leaf-stalk lacks milky juice. Autumn colouring
yellow, orange or red.
Flowers: Apr, at same time as the leaves, unisexual, dangling in clusters
on long, limp stalks. Calyx bell-shaped, yellow-green; corolla absent.
Fruit: Aug-Sep, paired winged fruit, wings set at acute angle or parallel.
Bark: Grey, cracked (photo p. 248)
Distribution: E and C North
America. Grown in parks and
gardens in Europe. In collections
and large gardens throughout BI,
but not common.
Habitat: Rich, damp, loamy soils;
extreme shade species. Hardy
Similar species: Norway Maple
(p. 108).
Note: In North America the sap of
this species is used to make Maple
Syrup.

Sugar Maple: leaf lobes have long terminal
points and few, large teeth; the separations
between the lobes are rounded

Heldreich's Maple

Acer heldreichii

(Maple Family)

Shape: Small deciduous tree growing to about 15 m.
Leaves: Opposite, to 14 cm long and about the same width, often divided
almost to the base between 3 main lobes, with irregularly toothed margin.
Bright green above, pale yellow or grey-green below. Autumn colour gold.
Fruit: Aug-Sep, winged fruit, wings set at an acute angle or almost
parallel, sometimes curved and overlapping.
Distribution: Greece, Balkans. Occasionally planted as a park tree in
Europe. Rarely planted in BI.
Habitat: Mountain woodland.
Similar species: Sycamore (p. 106).

Heldreich's Maple: shoot with leaves

Silver Maple ❀ ☞

Acer saccharinum

(Maple Family)

Shape: Often multi-trunked deciduous tree with an irregular crown, growing to about 35 m in its natural habitat and up to about 20 m in Europe. Branches angled steeply upwards, and usually drooping towards the tips. Leaves opposite. Stalk lacking milky juice. Blade 8-16 cm long and deeply 5-lobed. Lobes narrowly pointed and themselves deeply toothed or lobed; silvery-white beneath.

Flowers: Feb-Apr, before the leaves, unisexual, yellow-green; male and female flowers in separate short-stalked dense clusters (on same or different plants).

Fruit: May-Jun, pale brown paired winged fruit. Wings each about 3.5 cm long, often curved and set more or less at right angles to each other.

Distribution: E and C North America. Planted along roads, in parks and large gardens.

Habitat: Prefers moist, occasionally flooded soil, near to water; hardy, light-loving species.

Silver Maple: leaf, showing deeply cut lobes

Silver Maple: shoot with fresh leaves

Cappadocian Maple ❀

Acer cappadocicum

(Maple Family)

Shape: Medium-sized deciduous tree growing to 20 m.

Leaves: Opposite. Blade 8-14 cm wide, with 5-7 pointed, entire lobes.

Fruit: Oct, wings spreading almost horizontal.

Distribution: Caucasus, W Asia to the Himalayas, W China. Occasionally grown in parks in Europe. In BI mainly in large gardens in W, and occasionally as street tree.

Habitat: Mixed broadleaved woodland, woodland edges.

Cappadocian Maple: cluster of fruits

Cappadocian Maple: leaf showing narrow, pointed lobes with entire margins

Smooth Japanese Maple 🌸☞
(Maple Family)   *Acer palmatum*

Shape: Small, round-crowned deciduous tree or shrub to 8(15) m tall.
Leaves: Opposite. Shape and colour very variable, typically to 10 cm long
and about the same width, with 5-7(9) sharply-toothed, tapering lobes.
Bright green at first, turning yellow, orange or purplish-red in the autumn.
Fruit: Oct-Nov, pairs of winged fruits with wings widely spread.
Bark: See photo p. 249.
Distribution: China, Japan, Korea. Widely planted as an ornamental in
gardens.
Habitat: On rich, not too damp soils; hardy.
Note: There are many garden forms of this species. Amongst the
commoner are 'Atropurpureum' (with dark, almost blackish-red leaves)
and 'Dissectum' (leaves divided right to the base; lobes very narrow,
almost feathery).

Many garden forms of the Smooth Japanese Maple have red foliage,
including opposite (below) 'Dissectum Ornatum'.

Smooth Japanese Maple: shoot with leaves
and young fruit

Smooth Japanese Maple: fruits of
red-leaved form

Amur Maple 🌸
(Maple Family)   *Acer ginnala*

Shape: Deciduous shrub or small tree to 6 m.
Leaves: Opposite, 4-9 cm long, 3-6 cm wide. 3-lobed or sometimes
5-lobed; central lobe with long, pointed tip. Leaf margin doubly toothed.
Bright red autumn colour.
Fruit: Jul-Aug, Wings set at an acute angle, or parallel.
Distribution: China, Japan, Korea, Manchuria. Planted as a hardy
decorative shrub in Europe;
occasionally in BI.

Amur Maple: shoot with clusters of fruits

Buckthorn *

Rhamnus cathartica

(Buckthorn Family)

Shape: Bushy deciduous shrub or small, rounded tree to 8 m tall.
Shoot: Often ending in a spine.
Leaves: Opposite. Stalk 1-2.5 cm long; blade broadly elliptical, 3-6(9) cm long, with a short point. Leaf margin finely toothed, usually hairless. Leaves have 3-4(5) pairs of curved veins which join together towards the tip.
Flowers: May-Jun, in groups of 2-8, in the leaf axils. Perianth 4-partite, yellow-green, small and inconspicuous.
Fruit: Aug-Oct, round, pea-sized, berry-like fruit with 2-4 seeds, blue-black and juicy when ripe. Poisonous.
Bark: Grey-brown to blackish, cracked (photo p. 249).
Distribution: Europe, W Asia, NW Africa.
Habitat: From lowland to hills (Alps to 1300 m), in scrub, hedges and woodland edges. Prefers calcareous soils. Light-loving or semi-shade species.
Similar species: Alder Buckthorn° (*Frangula alnus*) is closely related and a common deciduous shrub. Its main features are as follows:.
Shoot: Lacking thorns and with many pale, longitudinal corky projections.
Leaves: Alternate, entire, with 6-10 pairs of lateral veins.
Flowers: May-Sep, hermaphrodite, 5-partite, greenish white.
Fruit: July-Sep, ripen from green, through red to black.
Distribution: Europe, Turkey, NW Africa.
Habitat: Hedges and damp woodland, mainly on deep, boggy, acid soils.
The photographs opposite show (above) Buckthorn growing in a park and (below) in a more natural habitat.

Buckthorn: spine-tipped shoot, showing veins of finely-toothed leaves curving and joining towards tip (l); ripening fruits (r)

Buckthorn: flowering shoot

Alder Buckthorn: twig with ripening fruits, showing leaves with entire margins (l); twigs with typical longitudinal corky projections (r)

Cornelian Cherry ✿

Cornus mas

(Dogwood Family)

Shape: Deciduous shrub or small, rounded tree to 8 m tall.

Buds: Leaf buds elongate and pointed; flower buds stalked and rounded.

Leaves: Opposite. Stalk 5-10 mm long, blade oval to elliptic, with obvious pointed tip, 5-10 cm long, and with entire margins. Leaf surface shows 3-5 pairs of curved veins. Finely hairy on both sides.

Flowers: Feb-Apr, before the leaves (see photo opposite), in small clusters, 1-2 cm across with 4 scale-leaves at the base. Flowers hermaphrodite, with bright yellow 4-partite perianth.

Fruit: Aug-Sep, bright red, oval, berry-like fruit, with a 2-seeded stone. Flesh juicy, edible and sour-tasting.

Bark: Grey-brown, flaky.

Distribution: Central S Europe, Turkey, Caucasus. In BI introduced, mainly scattered in S.

Habitat: Warm, dry open oak woods, woodland edges, and scrub, on rich, calcareous soils. Often grown for its early bright flowers. Light-loving to semi-shade species.

Similar species: Dogwood ° (*Cornus sanguinea*) is a closely related deciduous shrub, native to Europe including BI. It differs in the following:

Shoot: Red in winter. *Leaves:* Turning red in the autumn.

Flowers: May-Jun, in terminal clusters, white.

Fruit: Sept, round, pea-sized, blue-black with a red stalk.

Habitat: Broadleaved woods, river valleys woods, woodland edges and scrub, on dry to moist, mainly calcareous, loamy soils.

Cornelian Cherry: shoot showing opposite leaves

Cornelian Cherry: the rounded, stalked flower buds are visible by late summer (l); these open into small clusters of flowers in early spring (r)

Cornelian Cherry: ripening fruits

Dogwood: the red-stalked clusters of shiny black fruits are characteristic

Phillyrea ☺ ☞

(Olive Family)

Phillyrea latifolia

Shape: Spreading, evergreen broadleaved tree to 10 m tall.

Leaves: Opposite, ovate to lanceolate, evergreen, leathery, smooth and glossy. Dark green above, paler beneath. Shallowly toothed from middle to tip.

Flowers: Apr-Jun, clustered in leaf axils. Very small and greenish-white. The most obvious feature are the bright yellow anthers which hide the rest of the flower.

Fruit: Small, round berry, about 1 cm across, blue-black.

Bark: Smooth, pale grey, cracking with age.

Distribution: S Europe, Mediterranean region. In BI uncommonly planted, mainly in S England.

Habitat: Evergreen oak woods, maquis.

Similar species: Resembles small tree of Holm Oak (p. 182), especially from a distance.

Note: An important species in remnants of Mediterranean woodland and maquis in S Europe.

Phillyrea: shoot with flowers and leaves

Olive ☞

(Olive Family)

Olea europaea

Shape: Small evergreen broadleaved tree, to about 10 m tall, often with twisted growth. Trunk short, branching from quite low down, thick and knotted in old specimens. Crown broad and irregularly branched.

Leaves: Opposite, evergreen, leathery. Narrowly elliptical to lanceolate (willow-like), 4-8 cm long, with entire margins (margins often slightly furled). Dark or grey-green above and smooth or slightly hairy; dense covering of silver-grey hairs beneath.

Flowers: Apr-Jul, in panicles in leaf axils. Hermaphrodite, small, calyx 4-toothed, corolla white, 4-lobed; 2 stamens; short 2-branched stigma. Pleasantly scented.

Fruit: Sep-Oct, the well-known olive, a drupe, to 4 cm long, with hard, rough stone surrounded by edible, oily flesh. At first green, usually ripening to black (but some remain green).

Bark: Pale grey, cracked.

Distribution: Mediterranean region, cultivated in many parts of the world with similar climate.

Habitat: Dry, warm sites. Olive groves usually planted on deep, rich soils. Drought-resistant, damaged by hard winters or late frosts. Requires full sun.

Note: An important species in remnants of Mediterranean woodland and maquis in S Europe. Ancient cultivated plant, mainly for its oil, and wood.

Olive: grey-green opposite leaves (l); fruits (r)

Paulownia ⊛
Foxglove Tree

Paulownia tomentosa

(Figwort Family)

Shape: Medium-sized broad-crowned deciduous tree growing to a height of about 15(20) m; rapid-growing.

Leaves: Opposite, very large, stalk 8-20 cm, blade 15-35 cm long and up to 30 cm wide. Leaves growing up from sucker shoots are even larger. Oval, with heart-shaped base, pointed at the tip, with entire margins and occasionally a small number of large teeth or weakly-developed lobes (especially on the larger leaves); hairy on both sides.

Flowers: Apr-May, before the leaves open, the rounded flower buds, which are covered with brown, felty hairs, are visible from late summer of the previous year. Flowers in upright panicles. Each flower is hermaphrodite and trumpet-shaped with a rather bell-like corolla tube with 5 unequal lobes. Violet or pale whitish violet, with yellow streaks inside; fragrant.

Fruit: Aug-Oct, leathery brown oval capsule 2-4 cm long, with a short beak; many small, winged seeds. The ripe capsules remain on the tree for a long time.

Bark: Smooth and grey-brown, sometimes with longitudinal streaks (photo p. 249).

Distribution: China. Commonly grown in S Europe and occasionally further N. In BI mainly in large gardens in the S.

Habitat: Rich, moist soils; in continental Europe grows best in the wine-growing regions, since it is particularly frost-sensitive when young. Older trees relatively hardy.

Similar species: Indian Bean Tree (p. 126).

Note: Paulownia is the only tree genus in the Figwort family, which consists mainly of herbs such as Figwort and Foxglove.

The photographs opposite show Paulownia with impressive flowers in spring (above) and large leaves in summer (below).

Shoot showing large, long-stalked leaves

Flower buds, showing brown, felty hairs (l); inflorescence, showing foxglove-like flowers

Oval fruit capsules, some open

124

Indian Bean Tree ✿

Catalpa bignonioides

(Bignonia Family)

Shape: Medium-sized deciduous tree growing to 15(20) m tall. Trunk usually rather short and crown broad.

Leaves: Opposite or in whorls of 3, very large; leaf-stalk 10-17 cm long, blade 10-25 cm long and 8-15 cm wide, pointed, broadly oval with heart-shaped base and entire margins. Young leaves softly hairy on both sides, later only on the paler underside. Foliage has unpleasant smell when crushed. Leaves open late, and fall early in the autumn.

Flowers: Jun-Jul, after the leaves, in upright, terminal, conical panicles. Individual flowers hermaphrodite, 3-5 across. Corolla tube bell-like, with 5 unequal lobes, white, striped yellow inside and speckled violet; weakly scented.

Fruit: Sep-Oct, slender, bean-like pods to 20-40 cm long and about 1 cm wide, rounded in cross section. These contain many small, flat seeds with pointed, hairy wings. The ripe capsules remain on the tree into the following spring.

Bark: Thin, grey-brown and flaky.

Distribution: SE North America. Common in S Europe and scattered as an ornamental tree elsewhere in Europe. In Britain grows best in the S.

Habitat: Lowlands, on rich, moist soils. Fairly hardy, but susceptible to late frosts and should therefore be planted only in mild, protected sites.

Similar species: Paulownia (p. 124).

Note: In recent years the hybrid *Catalpa* x *erubescens*, a cross between *C. bignonioides* and the Far Eastern *C. ovata*, has become very popular

as a garden tree in the British Isles. It is very floriferous, and the leaves, unlike those of *C. bignonioides*, regularly show 3-5 shallow, pointed lobes.

The photograph opposite shows Indian Bean Tree in fruit.

Catalpa x *erubescens*, showing leaves with shallow, pointed lobes

Indian Bean Tree: upright inflorescences

Indian Bean Tree: the bean-shaped fruits stay on the tree until the following year

Ginkgo ❀
Maidenhair Tree

Ginkgo biloba

(Ginkgo Family)

Shape: Deciduous tree growing to 30 m tall, with an irregular much-branched crown, narrow in young trees, broadening with age.
Leaves: Solitary and alternate on long shoots, arranged in small whorls (usually of 3) on newer shoots. Leaves fan-shaped, 5-8 cm across, long-stalked and with a leathery texture. Veins parallel, radiating out from base of leaf. Outer edge of leaf undulating or notched, often with a deep central notch dividing leaf into 2 lobes. Leaves pale green at first, later turning dark green and yellow in the autumn.
Flowers: Apr-May, at the same time as leaves, tree dioecious. Male flowers in catkin-like clusters of 2-5, 4-7 cm long, yellow, with many stamens. Female flowers long-stalked in groups of 1-3, green.
Fruit: Oct-Nov, fleshy, plum-like, yellow-green, ripening to yellow-orange, with an unpleasant smell.
Bark: Grey-brown at first, later ridged (photo p. 249).
Distribution: SE China. Common park and garden tree in Europe. In BI mainly in S England.
Habitat: Mixed woods at about 750 m. A hardy light-loving species, relatively insensitive to air pollution.
Notes: 1) Ginkgo is a so-called living fossil and is the only living representative of its family, which reached its peak over a hundred million years ago.
2) Despite its broad leaves and deciduous habit, this species is not an angiosperm, but belongs with the conifers to the gymnosperm group.
3) Most planted trees are male, partly because the female tree produces seeds which smell unpleasant when ripe.

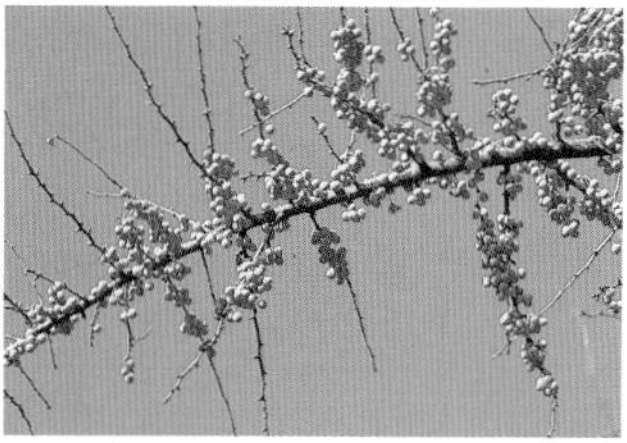

Branch with plum-like seeds; these have an unpleasant smell

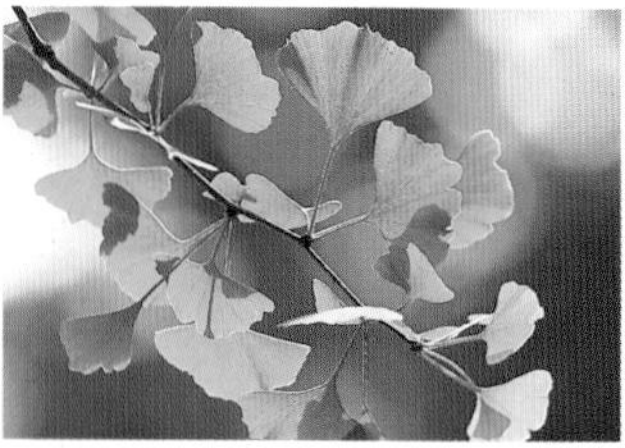

Shoot with leaves

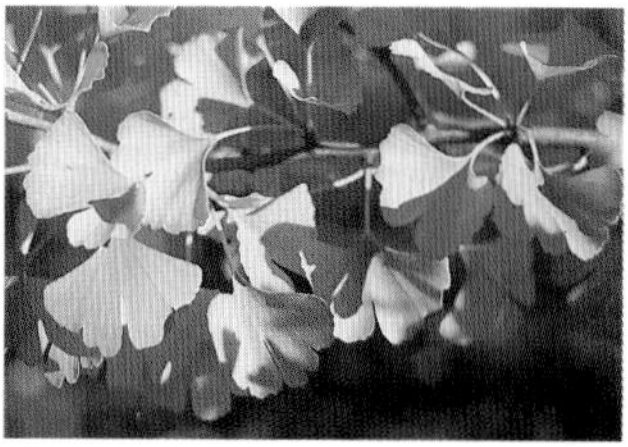

Leaves in autumn

Black Poplar *⊛

Populus nigra

(Willow Family)

Shape: Tall, rapidly-growing deciduous tree to 35 m. Crown broad and spreading, with strong branches.

Shoot: Hairless, shiny and yellowish.

Leaves: Alternate, stalks 2-6 cm long, blade triangular to wedge-shaped, pointed, 5-10 cm long, with a toothed margin. Hairless, dark green above and pale green below.

Flowers: Mar-Apr, before the leaves, flower bracts slit, lacking whiskers. Male flowers in dense hanging catkins to 9 cm long, yellow-brown or reddish. Female flowers in narrower yellow-green catkins, elongating in fruit.

Fruit: May-Jun, 2-celled capsules. Seeds (larger than those of White Poplar and Aspen) are white and woolly.

Bark: Smooth and pale grey at first, becoming ridged and blackish (photo p. 249).

Distribution: Mainly C, S and E Europe, Asia, W Siberia, N Africa.

Habitat: Wet woodlands, on damp, wet, or flooded fertile and base-rich sand and loam soils. Somewhat warmth-loving, shallow-rooted and drought-sensitive. Sends out suckers from base. In continental Europe often associated with White Poplar in mixed river-valley woods. Widely planted outside native range.

Notes: 1) The Lombardy Poplar ⊛, *Populus nigra* 'Italica', is an upright form which is very commonly planted along roads and as a windbreak. This has almost vertical branches and a narrow growth-form. Male trees are most commonly planted and reproduce from cuttings.

2) Many hybrid Poplars are also planted. These are usually hybrids between the Black Poplar and the closely related Cottonwood (*Populus deltoides*), a native of North America. They are usually referred to as *P. x canadensis* or *P. x euramericana*. There are many cultivars with different characters and members of this group are rather difficult to distinguish.

3) The British Isles has its own special form of Black Poplar ° (*P. nigra* ssp. *betulifolia*), which is confined to N and W Europe. It is a very large tree with deeply fissured bark with characteristic burrs on the trunk and branches.

4) All poplar species are dioecious – that is the whole tree is either male or female.

The photographs opposite show Lombardy Poplar (above left), British Black Poplar (above right), and Black Poplars in the open countryside where they are often planted (below).

Shoot with leaves

Fruiting catkins (l); the wind-dispersed tiny seeds are surrounded by woolly hair (r)

White Poplar ✿

(Willow Family)

Populus alba

Shape: Rapidly-growing deciduous tree to 35 m tall with a broad, open, strongly-branched crown.

Shoot: New growth covered with white felty hairs.

Leaves: Alternate, stalked, 2-4 cm long, hairy. Shape of leaf-blade very variable, from rounded to oval. Stronger shoots with leaves lobed rather like those of a maple. Leaves 4-10 cm long, often much larger on sucker shoots. Leaf-margins irregularly toothed. Upper surface of leaf at first with waxy bloom, later smooth and shiny green; lower surface retaining a covering of dense, white hairs.

Flowers: Mar-Apr, before the leaves, flower bracts toothed and with shaggy hairs. Male flowers in dense, drooping catkins, to about 8 cm long, grey and red, becoming paler. Female flowers in shorter, more slender catkins, yellow-green.

Fruit: May-Jun, 2-celled capsules, seeds very small and woolly.

Bark: Grey-white, smooth, darker and ridged towards base.

Distribution: S, C and E Europe, W Siberia, W Asia, N Africa. Introduced to BI, and often planted and naturalized, especially on dunes near coast.

Habitat: River valley woodland, often associated with oaks, elms and Ash. Prefers moist or wet soils subject to occasional flooding. Mainly on rich basic, sand, loam, or clay soils. Drought-tolerant, shallow-rooting, light-loving, pioneer species. Readily grows up from suckers. Widely planted as an ornamental tree and also naturalized.

Similar species: Grey Poplar (p. 136).

Leaf: green upper surface (l); white felty lower surface (r)

Shoot with leaves

Leaves are variable, with unlobed leaves (l) on the same tree as lobed leaves; ♂ catkins (r)

Aspen *

Populus tremula

(Willow Family)

Shape: Quick-growing deciduous tree, to 30 m tall, with broad, open crown.

Shoot: Hairless, shiny, yellow-brown.

Leaves: Alternate. Leaf-stalks laterally flattened and about the same length as blade. Blade 3-8 cm across, rounded to oval, hairy when young, later hairless. Shiny green above, paler beneath. Leaves on main shoots larger (to 15 cm), oval to triangular, relatively short-stalked.

Flowers: Mar-Apr, before the leaves, flower-bracts split, and densely whiskered. Male flowers in dense, dangling catkins to 11 cm long, at first reddish, becoming paler. Female flowers in reddish catkins of similar length..

Fruit: May-June, 2-celled capsules; seeds very small, with cottony hairs.

Bark: Grey-green at first, becoming darker and ridged towards the base in older trees.

Distribution: Europe, N Africa, Turkey, Siberia.

Habitat: From lowlands to montane regions (Alps to 2000 m); common in woodland clearings and at the edges of woods, in abandoned quarries and gravel workings, and on wasteland. Also forms woods in Eastern Europe. Tolerates wide range of soils, growing on calcareous as well as silicious soils. Prefers moist, rather fertile soils. Also colonizes poor, dry, rocky soils as a pioneer species. Hardy, drought-sensitive, relatively deep-rooted, light-loving species. Readily suckers.

Similar species: Grey Poplar (p. 136).

Note: The flattened leaf-stalks allow the leaf-blades to flutter and rustle in the wind. This means Aspens can often be heard before they are seen in dense woodland.

The photographs opposite show Aspens in winter (above) and in summer (below).

Leaves fluttering in the breeze in the crown of a young tree

Branch of ♂ tree with flowering catkins

Leaf, showing long, laterally flattened stalk (l); old ♂ catkins (r)

134

Grey Poplar ✿ ☞   *Populus canescens*

(Willow Family)

Shape: Deciduous tree to 35 m tall. Resembles White Poplar, but grows even more rapidly and somewhat taller.

Leaves. Alternate. Variable in size and shape, 4-10(15) cm long on short shoots, rather rounded to oval, not lobed, and with rounded teeth. On longer shoots more or less weakly lobed. Undersides of leaves covered with grey felty hairs, smooth and glossy dark green above.

Flowers and Fruits: Like those of White Poplar.

Bark: (photo p. 249).

Distribution: C and S Europe and W Asia. Introduced to BI and much planted.

Habitat: River valleys. Commonly planted in parks and along roads; wide tolerance.

Similar species: White Poplar (p. 132), Aspen (p. 134).

Note: Grey Poplar is a natural hybrid between White Poplar and Aspen. It is very variable, and there are many intermediate forms between the two parents.

The photographs opposite show Grey Poplar in summer (above) and in winter (below).

Grey Poplar: shoot with leaves

Grey Poplar: branches in leaf

Western Balsam Poplar ✿   *Populus trichocarpa*

(Willow Family)

This species, which is a native of W North America, is one of a group of poplars known collectively as balsam poplars because of the strong resinous scent of their buds on opening in the spring. Balsam poplars are now widely planted in Europe, particularly in the British Isles. This species, which grows to about 30 m, has ovate, pointed leaves not heart-shaped at the base and with more or less entire margins.

Western Balsam Poplar: young leaves emerging from sticky, aromatic buds

Sallow *
Pussy Willow
Goat Willow

Salix caprea

(Willow Family)

Shape: Small deciduous tree or shrub to about 12 m tall.

Shoot: Greenish- or reddish-brown, hairy at first, later hairless.

Leaves: Alternate, elliptical, with short oblique point, 4-10 cm long and about 5 cm broad, margins shallowly notched or entire. Leaf hairy above and somewhat shiny, becoming hairless; grey or blue-green and softly hairy below, with prominent veins. Stalk 1-2 cm long, hairy; stipules inconspicuous.

Flowers: Mar-Apr, before the leaves, male flower buds have silvery hairs for some weeks before the bright yellow stamens emerge. These miniature catkins are only 2-4 cm long. Female catkins greenish, lengthening after flowering. Nectar-producing, and good for early bees.

Fruit: May-Jun, elongated 2-celled capsule; seeds very small and hairy.

Bark: Smooth and grey at first, with large diamond-shaped corky warts, becoming ridged.

Distribution: Europe, Siberia, Turkey, S and E Asia.

Habitat: From lowlands right up into mountains (Alps to 2000 m). Woodland edges, also a pioneer tree species in clearings and on wasteland, gravel workings and quarries. Prefers rich, damp or somewhat dry soils, and also humus-poor, raw soils. Light-loving species.

Similar species: Grey Willow (p. 140).

Note: All willow species are dioecious (whole tree is either male or female). The photographs opposite show silvery white young catkins (above) and how Sallow may be densely and irregularly branching (below).

Leaves, showing grey-green underside with prominent veins

The fruits ripen to release fluffy seeds which may be carried long distances in the wind

Leaves

♂ catkins

White Willow *⊛☞

(Willow Family)

Salix alba

Shape: Broad-leaved tree growing to 28 m tall.

Leaves: Alternate, lanceolate and tapering, 5-10 cm long, finely-toothed, with a thick covering of silky, silvery hairs either on both surfaces or just on the undersides. Stipules small and falling off early.

Flowers: Apr-May, with the leaves, catkins stalked, 3-6 cm long, slender.

Bark: Deeply fissured (photo p. 249).

Distribution: Europe, W Siberia, W and SW Asia, Africa.

Habitat: Lowland sites, with warm summers, usually near water. Dominates in certain types of river valley woodland. Prefers fertile, usually calcareous soils which are wet for at least part of the year.

Similar species: Crack Willow (p. 144).

Note: There are various weeping willows related to the White Willow. The true Weeping Willow, *S. babylonica*, from China, is very rare in Europe, but hybrids with White Willow and Crack Willow are common. The commonest is *Salix* x *sepulcralis*, a hybrid with White Willow; it has yellow, drooping shoots. Another is Weeping Crack Willow, *S.* x *pendulina*.

The photographs opposite show White Willow: weeping form (above) and normal form (below).

White Willow: the ♂ catkins grow on leafy stalks

White Willow: winter twigs of normal (l) and weeping (r) forms

Grey Willow *

(Willow Family)

Salix cinerea

Shape: Shrub or small tree to 6(15) m tall.

Shoot: Blackish-grey and softly hairy.

Leaves: Alternate, elliptical, 6-10 cm long, pointed, with finely-toothed or entire margin. Green above, grey-green and softly hairy below.

Flowers: Like those of Sallow. Anthers often red before opening.

Distribution: Europe, W Siberia.

Habitat: Scrub, on damp or flooded soils; fens and bogs, streamsides, damp meadows.

Similar species: Sallow (p. 138).

Grey Willow: winter twigs (l); ♂ catkins (r)

Common Osier ❀ 🌸 ☞

(Willow Family)

Salix viminalis

Shape: Broad-leaved tree or shrub to 20 m tall with long, flexible cane-like twigs. Often pollarded (cut back regularly) to stimulate production of canes.

Leaves: Alternate, narrowly lanceolate and tapering, to 20 cm long and up to 2 cm wide, rolling over at the edges and usually with entire margins. Underside of leaves covered with silky white hairs and with prominent midrib and veins. Stipules falling off early.

Flowers: Mar-Apr, immediately before the leaves appear, catkins cylindrical and about 3 cm long, silkily hairy before opening. Anthers yellow; style and stigmas of female flowers feathery and pale yellow.

Distribution: Europe. Common in lowland BI

Habitat: Mainly lowlands alongside rivers and ditches, and in wet scrub. Prefers rich calcareous soils subject to flooding. Pioneer species. Widely planted as a source of canes for basketry.

Similar species: Olive Willow.

The photographs opposite show young trees (above) and an older tree showing dense regrowth after removal of twigs (below).

Common Osier: leading shoot

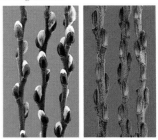

Common Osier: silky young catkins (l)
Olive Willow: winter twigs (r)

Olive Willow 🌸

(Willow Family)

Salix eleagnos

Shape: Broad-leaved tree or shrub to 20 m.

Leaves: Like those of Osier, but smaller (to 12 cm long) and often finely toothed towards the tip. Covered with matt, grey or white felty hairs beneath.

Flowers: Apr-May, catkins slender and usually twisted. Male catkins 3 cm long. Female catkins to 5 cm. In the male flowers the 2 filaments of the stamens are joined towards the base.

Distribution: Mountains of C and S Europe, Turkey. Occasionally planted in gardens in BI.

Habitat: A pioneer bush on banks and gravel in mountains. Calcareous soils subject to flooding.

Similar species: Osier.

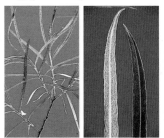

Olive Willow: shoot (l); leaf, showing grey felty hairs beneath (r)

Purple Willow ✱ ⊛ ☞
(Willow Family)

Salix purpurea

Shape: Shrub or small tree growing to 10 m tall. Twigs thin, cane-like, growing stiffly upright.

Shoot: Brown to red, hairless.

Leaves: Alternate, sometimes opposite. Lanceolate and pointed, wider in lower third of leaf. 4-12 cm long, up to 1.5 cm wide, finely-toothed towards the tip, hairless on both sides, always lacking stipules.

Flowers: Mar-Apr, before or with the leaves, catkins cylindrical, 1.4-1.5 cm long, often opposite. Male flowers each with 2 stamens with fully-fused filaments (look like a single stamen). Anthers at first purple-red, turning yellow.

Distribution: Europe, much of Asia, N Africa. Scattered in BI, often planted.

Habitat: Footpaths, ditches, river valley scrub. A pioneer species of sandy, muddy or gravelly soils subject to flooding.

Photographs opposite show release of fluffy seeds (above); shrub-like growth, with many thin upward-growing stems (below).

Purple Willow: ♂ catkins

Purple Willow: reddish-brown winter twigs (l); leaves (r)

Crack Willow ✱ ⊛
(Willow Family)

Salix fragilis

Shape: Deciduous tree growing to 20 m tall, often pollarded.

Shoot: Hairless, shiny, yellow-brown. Stems break (crack) easily at branch points.

Leaves: Alternate, lanceolate, long and tapering, to 17 cm long and 4 cm wide, toothed, shiny dark green above, paler below. Stipules fall away early.

Flowers: Mar-May, with the leaves, catkins stalked and slender, up to 6 cm long.

Distribution: Europe, W Siberia, SW Asia. Common in BI, wild and planted.

Habitat: Alongside rivers and streams. Usually on wet, fertile soils or those subject to occasional flooding.

Similar species: White Willow (p. 140), with which it often forms Hybrid Crack Willow, *Salix x rubens*, with a range of intermediate characters.

Crack Willow: winter twigs (l); leaves (r)

European Violet Willow 🏵

Salix daphnoides

(Willow Family)

Shape: Deciduous tree to 15 m tall.
Shoot: Usually shiny red, sometimes with a bluish bloom (hence the name).
Leaves: Alternate, lanceolate and pointed, 4-10 cm long, to 2.5 cm wide, finely toothed. Finely hairy at first, later becoming hairless, shiny dark green above, matt grey to bluish-green below. Stipules small, fused to the stalk..
Flowers: Mar-Apr, before the leaves, catkins covered with silvery, silky hairs before they open; 2-5 cm long and cylindrical.
Bark: Pale grey with weak longitudinal fissures (photo p. 249).
Distribution: Europe. Occasionally planted in BI; sometimes found in the wild (introduced).
Habitat: Mountains up to sub-alpine zone, along rivers and streams. On rich wet clay, sand, or gravel. Often planted in lowlands.

European Violet Willow: shoot with leaves

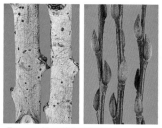

European Violet Willow: the twigs sometimes have a waxy bloom which rubs off (l); young twigs are often shiny red (r)

Bay Willow ✿ 🏵 ☞

Salix pentandra

(Willow Family)

Shape: Deciduous tree to 15 m tall.
Shoot: Usually shiny red-brown.
Leaves: Alternate, leathery, broadly lanceolate to elliptic, pointed. 5-10(15) cm long, 2-4 cm wide, hairless, finely toothed and glandular around margin (sticky). Shiny dark green above, matt pale green below. Leaf stalk with glands; usually lacks stipules.
Flowers: May-Jun, after the leaves, Catkins cylindrical, 2-5 cm long, on leafy stalks. Male catkins with 5 stamens.
Distribution: Europe to Caucasus and Siberia. In BI mainly in C and N as native plant.
Habitat: Wet bush and scrub, bogs; riversides. Damp peat or sandy or gravelly chalky soil. Popular ornamental species.

Bay Willow: shoot with fruiting catkins (l); leaf, showing small glands on stalk (r)

Silver Birch *⊛

Betula pendula

(Birch Family)

Shape: Quick-growing, oval-crowned deciduous tree to 30 m tall. Branches sharply angled upwards, and tending to curve downwards towards the tips.

Shoot: Hairless, shiny, red-brown, with numerous wart-like glands; sticky when young.

Leaves: Alternate. Stalk 1.5-3 cm long, hairless; blade triangular or wedge-shaped, tapering to a point, 4-7 cm long and doubly toothed; somewhat sticky when young.

Flowers: Apr-May, with the leaves, male and female flowers borne separately on the same tree. Male catkins yellow-brown and drooping, narrowly cylindrical and developing in the previous summer. At flowering time up to 10 cm long, unstalked. Female flowers in stalked slender green catkins, 2-4 cm long, erect when flowering, drooping in fruit.

Fruit: Jul-Sep, Small, 2-winged nutlets, each wing about 2-3 times as wide as the nutlet. Fruits between 3-lobed bracts in dense, brown catkins, falling from the tree and disintegrating (often with the help of birds) when ripe.

Bark: Shiny, reddish-brown at first, later turning pinkish or white with pale grey horizontal markings and dark grey scales; with deep fissures and knobbly bumps towards base of tree (photo p. 249).

Distribution: Europe, Siberia, Turkey, Caucasus, N Iran. In BI commoner towards the S; sometimes planted in streets.

Habitat: Mainly lowland, rarer in mountains (Alps to 1800 m); open, broadleaved and coniferous woodland, woodland edges, fens and bogs, heaths, wasteland. Tolerates a wide range of soil conditions but often restricted, through competition with other trees, to damp or dry sites on poor acid soils, often on sand. Hardy, a rather shallow-rooted, light-loving and pioneer species. Widespread in parks and along roads.

Similar species: Downy Birch (p. 150).

Note: See note on p. 150.

The photograph opposite shows an avenue of Silver Birch in autumn.

Branches with drooping tips

Fruiting catkins

Hairless shoot, showing pale, wart-like glands (l); leaf (r)

Downy Birch *
Hairy Birch

Betula pubescens

(Birch Family)

Shape: Medium-sized deciduous tree with oval crown, growing to 20 m tall. Branches stiff and angled sharply upwards, or horizontal, tips not usually curving down.

Shoot: Thickly covered with hairs right to the tip, later becoming hairless; very few warts or none at all.

Leaves: Alternate, relatively tough, stalk 1-2.5 cm long, hairy at least when young. Blade oval to diamond-shaped, rather rounded at the corners and usually rather less sharply pointed than those of Silver Birch. 3-5 cm long, singly or doubly-toothed; more or less hairless above, softly hairy below when young, later hairy only on the vein axils.

Flowers: Like those of Silver Birch.

Fruit: Jul-Sep, small, 2-winged nutlets, each wing not much wider than the nutlet. Fruits between 3-lobed bracts in dense, brown catkins, falling from the tree when ripe.

Bark: Red-brown at first, becoming greyish-white with brown or grey horizontal banding. Sometimes bark stays brownish even in large trees. Does not develop the black markings of Silver Birch.

Distribution: C, W and N Europe, Siberia, Caucasus. From the lowlands right up into the mountains (Alps to 2000 m); on boggy soils, and also in sub-alpine Larch/Arolla Pine communities close to the treeline. In Siberia forms woods over large areas. Even less demanding than Silver Birch, growing in damp and flooded conditions, on rich and poor soils, as well as on acid sand and peat bogs. In BI commoner towards the N; rarely planted. Avoids areas with dry air. Hardy, rather shallow-rooted, light-loving, pioneer species.

Similar species: Silver Birch (p. 148).

Note: Silver Birch and Downy Birch frequently hybridize with each other, producing intermediate forms which are difficult to identify.

The photograph opposite shows a group of Downy Birch in their natural habitat.

Leaves with fruiting catkins

Catkins open with the leaves (♂ catkins here)

River Birch
Black Birch ☞

Betula nigra

(Birch Family)

Shape: Deciduous tree to 30 m tall, often multi-trunked.

Leaves: Alternate. Leaf-stalk 7-17mm long, hairy; blade oval to diamond-shaped, pointed, 3-9 cm long, double-toothed, with 6-9 pairs of lateral veins. Bright shiny green above, grey-green and hairy beneath.

Flowers: Male catkins yellow, dangling, to 7.5 cm long; female catkins small, green and upright.

Bark: Red-brown, peeling into thin, shaggy flakes on young trees; dark brown and ridged with age (photo p. 249).

Distribution: E North America. In Europe as hardy park tree. In BI rarely planted; in a few larger gardens and parks in S England.

Habitat: Stream sides and wet woods.

Paper Birch
Canoe Birch

(Birch Family)   *Betula papyrifera*

Shape: Broad, rather conical deciduous tree, to about 40 m.

Leaves: Alternate. Stalk 1.5-2.5 cm long, hairy; blade oval, pointed, 5-10 cm long, double-toothed, with 6-9 pairs of side veins. Dark green above, yellow-green beneath; somewhat hairy on both sides when young, losing hairs later. Turning yellow and orange in autumn.

Flowers: Male catkins yellow and dangling, to 10 cm long; female catkins smaller, green and drooping.

Bark: Smooth, white, with horizontal dark lenticels; peels to reveal pink or orange colour beneath; only dark and cracked at base of old trunks.

Distribution: N North America. Hardy park tree in Europe. In BI uncommon; in some larger gardens and parks.

Habitat: Northern woods and mountains.

Himalayan Birch ❁

Betula utilis

(Birch Family)

Shape: Conical, deciduous tree to 25 m tall.

Leaves: Alternate, to about 10 cm long, toothed, tapering to a point. Dark glossy green above, with downy hairs on veins beneath. Turn golden yellow in autumn.

Flowers: Male catkins dangling, to about 15 cm; female catkins small, green and upright.

Bark: Papery, peeling; glossy orange-brown, or pinkish, sometimes pure white (var. *jacquemontii*) (photo p. 249).

Habitat: High mountain forests.

Distribution: China, Himalaya. In BI increasingly commonly planted in gardens, especially as the white-barked variety.

Himalayan Birch: fruiting catkin (l); bark (r)

Monarch Birch ☞

(Birch Family)

Betula maximowicziana

Shape: Deciduous tree growing to 30 m tall.

Leaves: Alternate. Stalk 2-4 cm long. Blade heart-shaped to oval (rather lime-like), pointed, large, (8-15 cm long, 5-10 cm wide), unevenly toothed and with 9-12 pairs of lateral veins, each vein ending in a marginal tooth. Leaves golden yellow in autumn.

Bark: Dark brown, later white or grey, can be orange-grey, with horizontal lenticels. Papery (photo p. 249).

Distribution: Japan. Hardy species, grown in parks in C Europe. In BI, found in some large gardens.

Monarch Birch: leaf and bark

Ermans Birch

(Birch Family)

Betula ermanii

Shape: Deciduous tree to 20 m tall.

Leaves: Alternate. Stalk glandular, 1-2.5 cm long; blade triangular to oval with rather a sharp point, 5-10 cm long, with coarse teeth and 7-11 pairs of lateral veins.

Bark: Smooth, yellowy-white, pinkish, or pure white, with horizontal lenticels; peeling into papery strips (photo p. 249)

Distribution: NE Asia, Japan. A hardy species sometimes grown in European parks and gardens. In BI rather rare, found in some large gardens and collections.

Ermans Birch: leaf and bark

Chinese Red-barked Birch

(Birch Family)

Betula albosinensis

Shape: Deciduous tree to 20 m tall.

Leaves: Alternate. Stalk 5-15 mm long; blade narrowly oval, with long tip, 5-9 cm long, doubly-toothed, with 10-14 pairs of lateral veins. Dark yellow-green above, with silky hairs on veins beneath.

Bark: Smooth, orange or reddish-brown, with pale horizontal lenticels. Peeling into thin, papery horizontal strips, revealing cream colour beneath (photo p. 249).

Distribution: C and W China. Hardy park tree in Europe. In BI rather rare, found in some large gardens and collections.

Chinese Red-barked Birch: leaf and bark

Common Alder *

Alnus glutinosa

(Birch Family)

Shape: Deciduous tree to 25(35) m tall. Trunk straight, reaching high into the crown. Often has more than one main trunk (see photos opposite).

Shoot: Hairless.

Leaves: Alternate. Leaf-stalk 2-3.5 cm long, blade rounded or obovate, 4-10 cm long, rounded or slightly concave at the tip, double-toothed, at first sticky, with 5-8 pairs of lateral veins. Hairs restricted to the vein axils on the undersides.

Flowers: Mar-Apr, before the leaves, male and female flowers on the same tree. Male catkins 6-12 cm long, drooping. Female catkins small, reddish-brown and stalked.

Fruit: Sep-Oct, small, flat, narrowly-winged nutlets in stalked, oval, brown, woody cones, 1-2 cm long. Cones usually stay on the tree right through the winter.

Bark: Smooth at first and shiny grey-brown, becoming dark grey to blackish brown, scaly and ridged (photo p. 250).

Distribution: Europe, Caucasus, Siberia and N Africa.

Habitat: Lowlands, more rarely in the mountains. Grows alongside streams and rivers and in damp deciduous woods. Prefers deep, mainly acid soils rich in humus, and subject to water-logging or occasional floods. Hardy, drought-sensitive, deep-rooted, light-loving species.

Similar species: Grey Alder (p. 158).

Note: Alders grow in symbiosis with certain bacteria (Actinomycetes), which absorb nitrogen from the air. These organisms live in nodules on the roots, and their presence means that alders tend to improve soil fertility.

Ripe cones; note stalks

Shoot with leaves

Buds are brownish violet, stalked and often sticky (l); the leaf usually has 5-8 pairs of lateral veins (r)

Grey Alder ✿ ☞

Alnus incana

(Birch Family)

Shape: Broadly conical deciduous tree to 15(25) m, usually many-trunked.

Shoot: Downy at first, becoming hairless later.

Leaves: Blade broad and elliptical, pointed, not sticky. 8-14 pairs of lateral veins. Grey-green and downy beneath. Otherwise like Common Alder.

Flowers: Feb-Apr, before main leaf growth, usually before Common Alder. Resemble those of Common Alder.

Fruit: Like Common Alder, but cones somewhat smaller, unstalked or with very short stalks.

Bark: Smooth, silver-grey (photo p. 250).

Distribution: N, C and E Europe, Caucasus. In BI introduced; planted in gardens and as shelter.

Habitat: Mountains. In C Europe in montane zone (500-1500 m); on mountain rivers and streams, wet slopes, sometimes flooded, rich, calcareous soils; unlike Common Alder avoids water-logged ground, and tolerates drier conditions. Hardy, quick-rooting pioneer species, suckering.

Similar species: Common Alder (p. 156).

Note: See note on p. 156.

Grey Alder: upper (l) & lower (r) surface of leaf; there are usually 8-14 pairs of lateral veins

Grey Alder: long, dangling ♂ catkins and inconspicuous stalkless ♀ flowers

Italian Alder ✿

Alnus cordata

(Birch Family)

Shape: Broadly conical deciduous tree, to about 25 m tall.

Leaves: Rounded, with heart-shaped base, to about 10 cm long, toothed. Dark, glossy green above, paler beneath, with hairs in vein axils. Comes into leaf early and holds leaves until late in season.

Flowers: Feb-Mar, Male catkins yellow, to 7.5 cm long; female catkins small, red, upright.

Fruit: Cone-like, woody, 3 cm long, green, ripening to brown.

Bark: Smooth, grey, developing shallow fissures with age.

Distribution: Corsica, C and S Italy. In BI commonly planted, especially in S.

Habitat: Deciduous woods in mountains.

Italian Alder: leaves and fruits

Hornbeam *⊛

Carpinus betulus

(Birch Family)

Shape: Deciduous tree growing to 25 m tall, with dense, rounded crown.

Leaves: Alternate, arranged in 2 rows. Stalk 5-15 mm long; blade ovate to oblong, with conspicuous veins, pointed, rounded or weakly heart-shaped at base, 5-11 cm long, double-toothed. Dark green and hairless above, paler beneath, with hairy vein axils. Lateral veins unbranched.

Flowers: May-Jun, appearing with the leaves, male and female flowers borne separately on the same plant. Males in drooping catkins, 4-7 cm long. Individual male flowers lack perianth and have 6-12 stamens. Female flowers in loose catkins at the ends of the shoots, 2-3 cm long. Individual female flowers with inconspicuous perianth and 2 feather-like stigmas.

Fruit: Oct, in loose, hanging clusters, to 15 cm long. Nutlets flat and oval, single-seeded and at the base of a 3-lobed bract. Fruits green at first, ripening to yellow-brown. Fruit dispersal from autumn through to spring.

Bark: Smooth, grey, similar to that of Beech, but fluted; cracking with age.

Distribution: Europe, Turkey, Caucasus, N Iran. In BI, native to SE England; frequently planted as hedge or roadside tree – often as pyramidal form.

Habitat: Lowlands in areas with relatively warm summers, only reaching about 800 m in the mountains. Forms mixed woods with Oak. Prefers moist to damp, rich, basic, loamy soils. Deep-rooting, semi-shade species. Common in parks and also used as a hedge since it tolerates regular cutting well.

Similar species: Hop Hornbeam (p. 162).

Shoot with fruits

Bark: smooth grey and fluted (l); leaf (r)

Young ♂ catkins (l); fruits (r)

Turkish Hazel ☞

Corylus colurna

(Birch Family)

Shape: Straight-trunked, deciduous tree growing to about 20 m tall with dense, conical crown.

Leaves: Like those of Hazel. Blade usually rather larger (7-15 cm long), stalk 2-6 cm long.

Flowers: Like Hazel.

Fruit: Sep-Oct, in clusters, nut about the same width as length, surrounded by a black, deeply-lobed bract. Seeds edible.

Bark: Grey, rough and scaly.

Distribution: SE Europe to W Asia. Planted in parks and along streets in C Europe. Rather uncommon in BI, mainly in parks and collections.

Habitat: Warm, mixed oak woodland. Hardy.

Similar species: Hazel (p. 164).

Turkish Hazel: leaves

Turkish Hazel: fruits, showing deeply lobed bracts

Hop Hornbeam ☞

Ostrya carpinifolia

(Birch Family)

Shape: Deciduous tree to 20 m tall.

Leaves: Like those of Hornbeam, but with some of the veins branching towards the margin.

Flowers: Apr-May, with the leaves, like Hornbeam but male catkins appearing in preceding summer, and to 12 cm long when in flower.

Fruit: Jul-Aug, in drooping, hop-like clusters. Nut enclosed in a bladder-like cream-coloured husk.

Bark: Smooth and grey at first (photo p. 250), later darkening and becoming flaky and ridged.

Distribution: SE and S Europe, as far N as S Alps, Turkey. In BI rarely planted; found in a few collections.

Habitat: Sub-mediterranean broadleaved mixed woodland and scrub, often with Downy Oak and Manna Ash. Prefers warm sites, on calcareous or silicious soils.

Similar species: Hornbeam (p. 160). The photograph opposite (below) shows fruiting shoots.

Hop Hornbeam: leaf (l); fruits (r)

Hazel ✻ ⊕ ☞

Corylus avellana

(Birch Family)

Shape: Deciduous shrub or small tree growing to about 6 m tall.
Leaves: Alternate. Stalk covered with glandular hairs and 5-15 mm long.
Blade rounded to broadly-obovate, pointed and heart-shaped at base,
6-13 cm long (often longer on powerful sucker shoots). Leaf-margin
doubly-toothed to weakly-lobed.
Flowers: Feb-Apr, before the leaves, male and female flowers on the
same plant. Male flowers in drooping catkins which appear during the
previous summer. Female flowers small, resembling leaf-buds, but with
feather-like red stigmas.
Fruit: Aug-Oct, single-seeded nuts, surrounded by a green involucre of overlapping bracts, about the same length as the nut. Seeds edible and rich in oil.
Bark: Smooth, grey-brown, often shiny, later cracked (photo p. 250).
Distribution: Europe, Turkey, Caucasus. Common native in BI,
sometimes planted in gardens as well.
Habitat: From the lowlands right up into the mountains, even
occasionally into the sub-alpine zone. Deciduous woods and scrub,
woodland clearings and hedges. Prefers moist, deep, fertile, loamy soils.
Shallow-rooted, semi-shade species. Widely spread through cultivation.
Similar species: Turkish Hazel (p. 162), Filbert.
The photos opposite show Hazel in flower (above), garden variety (below).

Hazel: leaf (l); ♂ catkins and bud-like group of ♀ flowers (r)

Hazel: cluster of fruits

Filbert ⊕

Corylus maxima

(Birch Family)

Differences from Hazel are as follows:
Leaves: Mostly larger.
Fruit: Involucre tube-shaped, enclosed, or split along one side and longer
than the nut, narrowing towards top.
Distribution: SE Europe, Turkey.
Cultivated in parts of Europe for its
edible nuts. In BI grown in gardens
and orchards, notably in Kent
(Kentish Cobs).
Similar species: Hazel.
Note: There is also a red-leaved form
of the Filbert with leaves and fruit
husks dark red.

Filbert: red-leaved form

164

Common Beech *⊛

Fagus sylvatica

(Beech Family)

Shape: Deciduous tree to 40 m tall. Solitary trees short-trunked and heavy-crowned; when growing in groups or closed stands taller and narrower with fewer branches, and with narrower crown.

Leaves: Alternate, in 2 rows. Stalk 1-1.5 cm long; blade oval to elliptic, pointed (5-10)15 cm, with 5-9 pairs of lateral veins. Margin wavy or weakly-toothed. Leaf covered with silky hairs at first, later hairless.

Flowers: End of Apr-May, with the leaves, flowers of both sexes on the same tree. Male flowers long-stalked, yellowish and dangling, each flower with 5-15 stamens. Female flowers in pairs, in short-stalked, upright, felty heads.

Fruit: Sep-Oct, paired, triangular, brown nutlets, each 1-2 cm long, inside a bristly, brown 4-lobed husk.

Bark: Silver-grey and remaining smooth (photo p. 250).

Distribution: W, C and S Europe. In BI, common and widely planted, sometimes as a hedge; probably native only locally in S England and Wales.

Habitat: Wide distribution in mixed broadleaved woodland and also as pure woods of Beech. From lowlands right up into the mountains (Alps to 1600 m). Best developed in the more oceanic areas (with moist and mild winters). Grows best in moist, reasonably deep, fertile, calcareous soils but also found growing on more acid soils. Sensitive to drought, flooding and late and winter frost. Deep-rooted shade species.

Similar species: Oriental Beech (p. 168).

The photograph opposite shows a fine, broad-crowned specimen in three seasons.

Narrow winter buds (l); leaf (r)

Flowers: ♂ (l), drooping; young female (r), upright

Common Beech: shoot with leaves

Beech flowers (♂ flowers shown here) open as the leaves appear

Oriental Beech

Fagus orientalis

(Beech Family)

Shape: In its native region a tall deciduous tree growing to 40 m; in N and C Europe usually to about 20 m. Usually has somewhat narrower growth than Common Beech.

Leaves: Like those of Common Beech but on average larger, with maximum width above the centre. Stalk and veins on the underside more or less hairy.

Fruit: Like Common Beech, but with basal bristles of the fruit husk more leaf-like.

Distribution: SE Europe, Turkey, N Iran, Caucasus. Hardy park tree in the rest of Europe. In BI a rare species found in certain collections.

Similar species: Common Beech (p. 166).

Note: There are many cultivated varieties of Common Beech. Amongst the commoner in parks and gardens are the following: Copper Beech 'Purpurea' (this covers many red-leaved forms); and 'Pendula' with drooping branches, often trailing on the ground.

The photographs opposite show Copper Beech (above) and Common Beech woodland (below).

Oriental Beech: leaf (l) - larger that that of Common Beech, with more lateral veins; ripening fruit (r)

Shoot of Copper Beech

Bristly husks, after release of 'beech nuts'

Sweet Chestnut ✿   *Castanea sativa*

(Beech Family)

Shape: Broad-crowned deciduous tree to about 30 m tall.

Leaves: Alternate, leathery. Stalk 1-2.5 cm long, blade narrowly elliptical to lanceolate, pointed, 10-25 cm long, edged with coarse, bristly teeth. Shiny dark green above, paler below with felty hairs when young, becoming hairless later.

Flowers: end of May-Jul, after the leaves have opened, male and female flowers on the same tree, clustered together, often on the same spike; both sexes small and creamy-yellow. Catkins erect, 10-25 cm long. Female flowers either solitary or in groups of 2 to 3, usually growing at the base of the male catkins and surrounded by a green scaly husk. Stigmas white, spreading.

Fruit: Oct, shiny brown, leathery, edible nut (the familiar chestnut) about 2-3 cm long. Up to 3 nuts enclosed in brownish-yellow spiny husk, opening into 4 sections when ripe.

Bark: Smooth and olive-brown at first, becoming grey-brown with vertical spiral ridges (photo p. 250).

Distribution: S Europe, Turkey, N Africa. Naturalized locally in S Europe. In BI planted throughout, especially in SE England.

Habitat: Sub-mediterranean mixed oak woodland in regions with mild winters, warm summers, and relatively high rainfall. Usually on silicious soils. Deep-rooting semi-shade species.

♂ catkins (l), ♀ flower (r), showing white stigmas protruding from scaly husk

Shoot showing long, upright ♂ catkins

Leaves

Fruits

Sessile Oak * ⊛

Quercus petraea

(Beech Family)

Shape: Deciduous tree growing to 30(40) m tall. Trunk usually straight and reaching high into the crown.

Crown: Broad, dense and more regular than English Oak.

Shoot: Hairless.

Leaves: Alternate. Leaf-stalk 1-3 cm long; blade obovate to elliptic, 6-16 cm long with a lobed margin. About 4-8 blunt or rarely somewhat pointed lobes on each side. Leaf base tapering, rounded or weakly heart-shaped. Leaf has beard-like hairs on the vein axils of the underside.

Flowers: May, appearing with the leaves, Unisexual, borne separately on the same plant. Male flowers in yellow-green, pendent catkins. Females in small, inconspicuous clusters of 1-6, usually with a reddish 3-lobed stigma.

Fruit: Sep-Oct, Short-stalked or sessile acorns in groups of 1-6. Acorns cylindrical, 2-3 cm long, with a scaly cup. at the base; green at first, ripening brown, without dark longitudinal bands.

Bark: Grey-green and smooth at first, later turning grey-brown with deep vertical ridges.

Distribution: W, C and S Europe, Caucasus. In BI throughout, especially in N and W.

Habitat: Broadleaved woods from lowland to montane, growing to higher altitudes than English Oak. Found on a wide range of soil types, but avoids wetter soils. Also found in sub-mediterranean broadleaved woods. This species has long been planted in forests and also in parks and towns. Deep-rooted, semi-shade species.

Similar species: English Oak (p. 174), Downy Oak (p. 176), Turkey Oak (p. 178). The photograph opposite shows an old Sessile Oak.

Leaf has a longer stalk than that of English Oak, with a larger number of more regular lobes, and usually tapers towards the base

Shoot

2 ripening acorns, showing short stalks

172

English Oak * ⊛
Pedunculate Oak

Quercus robur

(Beech Family)

Shape: Deciduous tree growing to 35(50) m tall. Trunk usually branching fairly low down. Crown somewhat irregular and spreading.

Leaves: Alternate, stalk only 2-10 mm long; blade obovate to wedge-shaped, 5-15 cm long, with 3-6 lobes at each side. Leaf-base more or less heart-shaped, with auricles. Leaf hairless on both sides.

Flowers: May, with the leaves; unisexual, borne separately on the same plant. Male flowers in drooping yellow-green catkins. Female flowers in inconspicuous stalked spikes of 1-6 flowers, usually with reddish, 3-lobed stigma.

Fruit: Sep-Oct, Acorns borne on long stalks (2-10 cm) in groups of 3(5). Acorns 2-3 cm long, surrounded by scaly cup for the lower third; green at first, ripening to brown, sometimes with dark longitudinal stripes.

Bark: Grey-green and somewhat shiny at first, becoming thick, grey-brown, and ridged (photo p. 250).

Distribution: Europe, Caucasus. In BI throughout

Habitat: Mixed broadleaved woodland, from lowland to montane levels. Common on wet or flooded soils along river valleys, but also on poor, acid soils, where it is often mixed with birch or pine. Long planted in woodland, parks and along streets. Deep-rooting, light-loving species.

Similar species: Sessile Oak (p. 172), Downy Oak (p. 176), Hungarian Oak (p. 176), Turkey Oak (p. 178).

Note: Trees (presumed hybrids) with intermediate characters often occur where Sessile Oak and English Oak are both found. Such hybrid trees are common in the British Isles.

Flowering shoot, the flowers open with the new leaves

♂ catkins, with inconspicuous red ♀ flowers above (l); acorns, showing long stalk (note auricles on leaf base) (r)

Shoot

Leaf, showing short stalk

Downy Oak ☞

Quercus pubescens

(Beech Family)

Shape: Broad-crowned tree to about 25 m tall, usually with somewhat twisted trunk; often a bush.

Shoot: Densely covered with fine hairs.

Leaves: Alternate. Stalk 8-15 mm long and hairy; blade obovate, 5-12 cm long, with 4-7 blunt lobes at each side, (lobes sometimes rather pointed). Base of leaf wedge-shaped or heart-shaped. Leaf at first hairy on both sides, later only on the grey-green undersides.

Flowers: Like those of Sessile Oak.

Fruit: Oct, in short-stalked clusters of 1-5. Acorns oval, pointed, usually smaller and slimmer than those of Sessile Oak. Cup scaly and downy, enclosing a third to half of the acorn.

Bark: Grey-brown, with deep furrows (photo p. 250).

Distribution: S, C and SW Europe, Turkey, Caucasus. Rarely grown in BI; only in a few collections.

Habitat: Warm sub-mediterranean broadleaved woodland. Usually on dry, fertile, calcareous soils. Also found as outliers on warm, dry cliffs in C Europe. Deep-rooted, light-loving species.

Similar species: Sessile Oak (p. 172), English Oak (p. 174), Turkey Oak (p. 178).

Downy Oak: shoot

Downy Oak: leaf: upper side (l); underside with downy hairs (r)

Hungarian Oak ✾

Quercus frainetto

(Beech Family)

Shape: Broad-crowned tree to 40 m tall.

Shoot: With grey hairs at first, quickly becoming hairless.

Leaves: Alternate, stalk 2-8 mm, blade obovate to elliptic and 10-20 cm long. Leaf margin with deep, narrow lobes, 7-10 on each side. Leaves hairy beneath.

Fruit: Oct, in short-stalked clusters of 1-5.

Distribution: S and SE Europe. Grown in parks elsewhere. In BI not commonly planted: large gardens in England and Ireland.

Habitat: Prefers sunny, dry hills.

Hungarian Oak leaf, showing short stalk and deeply divided lobes

Turkey Oak 🌸☞

Quercus cerris

(Beech Family)

Shape: Broadleaved tree growing to 35 m tall.
Shoot: Covered with grey felty hairs, becoming hairless.
Buds: With thread-like stipules.
Leaves: Alternate, leathery. Leaf stalk to 2 cm long; blade narrowly elliptic to obovate, 6-12(16) cm long, with 4-9 mostly pointed lobes on each side and a rounded to weakly heart-shaped base. Leaves rough on both surfaces, often felty and somewhat sticky beneath. Thread-like stipules remain until following season.
Fruit: Sep, in short-stalked clusters of 1-4. Acorn to 3 cm long, with up to half enclosed by cup. Cup has long, slender, thread-like scales. Ripening in Autumn of second year.
Bark: Hard, grey to blackish-brown, thick and deeply ridged (photo p. 250).
Distribution: S and SE Europe, Turkey. Grown in parks elsewhere. In BI often planted; naturalized on some areas of acid sand in the S.
Habitat: Sub-mediterranean oak woods on warm, not too dry, calcareous or silicious soils. Hardy.
Similar species: Sessile Oak(p. 172), English Oak(p. 174), Downy Oak (p. 176).

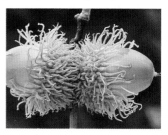

Turkey Oak: buds, showing feathery stipules (l); leaf (r)

Turkey Oak: acorns, showing cups with thread-like scales

Caucasian Oak

Quercus macranthera

(Beech Family)

Shape: Deciduous tree to 20 m tall.
Shoot: Grey and felty.
Leaves: Alternate. Stalk 1-2 cm long; blade obovate to elliptic, 6-18 cm long, with 8-11 lobes on each side. Leaf with grey felty hairs beneath. Stipules thread-like.
Distribution: Caucasus and N Iran. Grown in some large gardens and collections. Rather rarely planted in BI; some collections only.

Caucasian Oak: leaf (l); acorn (r)

Cork Oak ✿

Quercus suber

(Beech Family)

Shape: Short-trunked evergreen, broadleaved tree with a broad, open crown, growing to 15(20) m tall.

Leaves: Alternate, hard and leathery. Leaf stalk 5-15 mm long; blade oval to elliptic, 3-7 cm long with a rounded base. Margin with 4-6 sharp, pointed teeth on each side; sometimes entire. Hairless above and shiny dark green; grey felty hairs beneath. Often only hairy along veins.

Flowers: Like those of Holm Oak.

Fruit: Like those of Holm Oak, but acorn cup has elongated and somewhat spreading scales, covered in felty hairs.

Bark: Soft, grey and corky, becoming very thick and furrowed.

Distribution: Mediterranean region (originally mainly W Mediterranean). In BI occasionally planted in large gardens and parks, especially in S; but the Lucombe Oak, a hybrid between Cork Oak and Turkey Oak (p. 178), is much more commonly seen in BI.

Habitat: Open woods, often cultivated as a crop. Prefers stony, rather acid soils in warm, dry sites; very sensitive to frost.

Similar species: Holm Oak (p. 182)

Note: This species has long been cultivated for its corky bark. The young trees have a hard, not very elastic cork which is not harvested. This bark is removed when the trees are about 20 years old, after which they develop the valuable soft cork which is harvested at roughly 10-year intervals. The main centres of cork production are in Portugal and S Spain where cork plantations cover large areas of the countryside. Such woods are generally managed and thinned to promote the growth of the large, heavy-branched trees which give the best cork crop.

Ripening acorns: note slightly spreading scales

Fruiting twig

Corky bark

Holm Oak ✿

(Beech Family)

Quercus ilex

Shape: Evergreen broadleaved tree to 20 m tall. Often short-trunked and densely branching; commonly a shrub, particularly in the Mediterranean region.

Leaves: Thick and leathery. Leaf stalk 6-15 mm long; shape of blade very variable, oval or elliptical to lanceolate, 2-8 cm long, rounded towards the base. Margins may be entire or sharply toothed (like Holly). Dark green and shiny above, hairy when young, becoming hairless; softly hairy beneath.

Flowers: Apr-May, male and female flowers borne separately on the same tree. Male flowers in drooping yellow-green catkins. Females in short-stalked clusters, singly or in pairs (rarely in 3s), small and inconspicuous.

Fruit: Sep-Oct, short-stalked clusters of 1 or 2 acorns. Acorns narrowly oval to 3 cm long, cup enclosing from a third to a half of the acorn. Cup scales not spreading, softly hairy.

Bark: Grey-brown to black, rough and flaky.

Distribution: Mediterranean region (mainly W Mediterranean) as far N as the S Alps. A characteristic species of Mediterranean evergreen woods in areas with mild, damp winters and hot, dry summers. Widespread in maquis. Common on base-rich fertile soils, but not restricted to these. Widely planted in W Europe (north of its natural range), including the BI. Frost-sensitive so it grows best in milder climates near the coast.

Similar species: Cork oak (p. 180).

Note: Holm Oak is the natural woodland of much of the Mediterranean lowland. Only remnants of this woodland now remain, and most have been replaced by maquis scrub.

Note the dense rounded crown of the Holm Oak shown opposite.

Shoot with young acorns (note leaves here are entire)

Shiny, leathery, evergreen foliage

Leaf with sharply-toothed margin (NB leaves are variable)

182

Red Oak ✿

Quercus rubra

(Beech Family)

Shape: Fast-growing deciduous tree growing to 30(50) m tall. Crown conical at first, becoming broader and rounder with age.

Leaves: Alternate. Stalk 2-5 cm long; blade elliptical in outline, 10-25 cm long, 5-15 cm wide, wedge-shaped or rounded at the base. Margin with 4-6 irregularly-toothed lobes on each side. Dark green above, paler below. Autumn colour orange to scarlet.

Flowers: May, male and female flowers borne separately on the same tree. Male flowers in long yellow-green catkins. Female flowers small and inconspicuous, solitary or in pairs and sessile or very short-stalked.

Fruit: Oct, rather short, squat acorns to 2.5 cm, sessile or short-stalked, solitary or paired. Cup very shallow, covering less than a third of the reddish-brown acorn. Acorn reaches only about the size of a pea in the first year, ripening in the second autumn.

Bark: Grey, smooth (photo p. 250), later developing furrows.

Distribution: C and E North America, where it is a common woodland tree. Commonly planted in parks, gardens and along roads, also in some places as a forestry tree.

Habitat: Grows on poor, sandy soils as well as richer loamy soils, but dislikes shallow, wet, or very calcareous soils. Deep-rooting, light-loving species.

Similar species: Scarlet Oak, Pin Oak (p. 186).

Note the broad crown and heavy branches in the photographs opposite.

The flowers (here ♂ catkins) appear with the leaves

The squat acorns develop in flat, shallow cups

Autumn colours

Shoot (l) and leaf (r), showing toothed lobes

Scarlet Oak ⊕ ☞

Quercus coccinea

(Beech Family)

Shape: Quick-growing deciduous tree to 30 m tall with open, rounded crown.

Leaves: Alternate. Leaf-stalk 3-6 cm long; blade elliptical in outline, 8-18 cm long, on average smaller than leaf of Red Oak, but larger than leaf of Pin Oak. Leaf base narrow, broadly wedge-shaped. Leaves with 3, or more rarely 4, deep, narrow lobes on each side. Separations between lobes rather rounded in outline. Leaves shiny-green above, paler green beneath. Bright scarlet in Autumn.

Flowers: Like those of Red Oak.

Fruit: Oct, squat oval acorns, to 2.5 cm long; cup covering a third to half of acorn. Ripening in second Autumn.

Distribution: E and C North America. Grown as an ornamental tree in parks and gardens in Europe, including BI.

Habitat: Most commonly on poor, dry, acid soils.

Similar species: Red Oak (p. 184), Pin Oak.

Scarlet Oak: the leaves usually have 3 toothed lobes on each side, with deep rounded separations between

Pin Oak

Quercus palustris

(Beech Family)

Shape: Quick-growing deciduous tree to 30 m tall, with a broad, conical, or rounded crown, and a straight, tall trunk. Branches often horizontal, with many thin, upwardly-growing twigs.

Leaves: Like those of Scarlet Oak, but on average smaller and narrower.

Flowers: Like those of Red Oak.

Fruit: Oct, small oval acorns to about 1.2 cm. Ripening in second Autumn.

Distribution: NE and C North America. Grown in parks and gardens in Europe. Uncommon in BI, mainly in S England.

Habitat: Lowland, usually in flood plain of rivers on moist or wet soils.

Similar species: Red Oak (p. 184), Scarlet Oak.

Pin oak: shoot (l); leaf (r) (very similar to that of Scarlet Oak)

Wych Elm *⊛

Ulmus glabra

(Elm Family)

Shape: Deciduous tree to 40 m tall with a broad, rounded crown.

Leaves: Alternate, arranged in two rows. Leaf stalk short, only 3-6 mm long. Blade elliptical to obovate, 8-16 mm long, widest above the middle and usually more or less 3-pointed. Base asymmetric. Leaf margin toothed. Both sides of leaf rough and hairy.

Flowers: Like those of Small-leaved Elm, but perianth with rust-red whiskers, and reddish stigma.

Fruit: Like Small-leaved Elm fruits, but somewhat larger (2-3 cm long). Achene in centre of wings.

Bark: Smooth at first, becoming grey-brown and ridged later.

Distribution: Europe, Turkey, Caucasus. In BI mainly in N and W.

Habitat: Mixed deciduous woods, from the hills right up into the mountains (Alps to 1400 m), often with Beech, Sycamore, Ash and lime. Prefers damp, rich, loose, deep, basic soils in cool moist sites (e.g. ravines and shady slopes). Not sensitive to winter and late frosts; deep-rooting, semi-shade species. Often planted in parks and along roads.

Similar species: Small-leaved Elm (p. 190), European White Elm (p. 192).

Note: The naturally occurring hybrids between Wych Elm and Small-leaved Elm are known as Dutch Elms (*Ulmus* x *hollandica*). These trees show characters intermediate between the parents, and they are sometimes difficult to distinguish.

The small clusters of flowers appear before the leaves (l); fruits (r) - note that wing surrounds achene

Shoot

Winter Buds (l); leaf (r) has asymmetrical base and 3-pointed tip

Small-leaved Elm (and others) * ⊛

(Elm Family)   *Ulmus minor*

Shape: Deciduous tree growing to 30 m tall with a rounded crown. Very variable in shape, including shrub-like forms.

Leaves: Alternate, arranged in two rows. Very variable in size and shape. Stalk 5-15 mm long, blade elliptic with narrow point, 4-12 cm long with an asymmetrical base. Margin once or twice-toothed. Usually hairless above and shiny dark green; hairs restricted to vein axils beneath.

Flowers: Mar-Apr, before the leaves, hermaphrodite, in dense, many-flowered clusters. Individual flowers 3-5 mm long, short-stalked or sessile with inconspicuous perianth, 4-6 long stamens and whitish stigma.

Fruit: May-Jun, in clusters 1.5-2.5 cm long, short-stalked, hairless. Achenes flat and surrounded by skin-like wings, green at first, ripening to a yellow-brown.

Bark: Smooth when young, stems often with grey, corky ridges. Older bark grey-brown, with longitudinal and horizontal ridges.

Distribution: Europe (excluding Scandinavia), N Africa, Turkey, Caucasus

Habitat: Lowlands and hills. Mixed deciduous woodland, river valley woodland, woodland margins and fields. Deep, rich and basic soils, dry to moist (including those subject to occasional flooding). Warmth-loving, deep-rooting semi-shade species. Often planted in parks and along roads.

Similar species: Wych Elm (p. 188), European White Elm (p. 192).

Note: In addition to the hybrid Dutch Elm (see p. 188), there are a number of forms of this species, usually denoted as subspecies. These include ssp *minor* (= *Ulmus carpinifolia*) the Small-leaved Elm; ssp *angustifolia* the Cornish Elm; and the English Elm, *Ulmus procera* (= *Ulmus minor* var. *vulgaris*).

NB: Elm taxonomy is difficult, and the various forms have been interpreted in different ways. The photograph opposite shows Huntingdon Elms (a hybrid form) in spring.

The fruits develop before the leaves

Flowers (l); fruits (r)

Twigs with corky ridges (l); leaf (r), showing asymmetrical base

190

European White Elm

Ulmus laevis

(Elm Family)

Shape: Broad-crowned deciduous tree to 30 m tall.

Leaves: Alternate, arranged in 2 rows. Stalk 5-8 mm long; blade elliptic with prominent point, and 6-15 cm long. Leaf base markedly asymmetric. Margins twice-toothed, the larger teeth pointing forwards. Softly hairy on both sides at first, later losing the hairs from upper surface, grey-green and more or less hairy beneath.

Flowers: Like those of Small-leaved Elm, but with longer stalks and more open clusters.

Fruit: Like those of Small-leaved Elm, but smaller (1-1.5 cm long), and dangling on stalk to 2 cm long. Achenes in centre of winged fruit. Fruit wing has ciliate margin.

Bark: Grey-brown with a network of ridges (photo p. 250); also developing burrs.

Distribution: C, SE and E Europe, Turkey. Also planted in parks and along roads in C Europe. Very rarely grown in BI, only in a handful of collections.

Habitat: Mixed deciduous woodland in warmer, lowland sites (rarely above 600 m). Common in river valley woodlands on moist, wet or flooded, rich soils. Deep-rooting, semi-shade species.

Similar species: Wych Elm (p. 188), Small-leaved Elm (p. 190).

Note: So-called Dutch Elm disease attacks all three native Elms across various parts of Europe. It is caused by the fungus *Ceratocystis ulmi*. Afflicted trees show die-back of foliage and branches and are often killed.

Shoot

Whilst the normal winter buds are narrow and pointed, the flower buds are more rounded (l); the flowers dangle in clusters (r)

Caucasian Elm

Zelkova carpinifolia

(Elm Family)

Shape: Deciduous tree, often many-trunked, growing to 25 m tall, with branches sharply angled upwards. Crown dense, broadly oval.

Leaves: Alternate. Stalk 2-3 mm long. Blade oval to elliptic, pointed, 2-7 cm long with rounded or weakly heart-shaped base. Leaf margin coarsely toothed. Upper side of leaf somewhat rough, underside hairy, mainly along the veins.

Fruit: Short-stalked rounded nutlets about 9 mm across (rarely developed in BI).

Bark: Beech-like, grey and smooth; later becoming flaky.

Caucasian Elm: leaves

Distribution: Caucasus. Planted in parks in Europe. In BI occasionally planted in large gardens and parks.

Habitat: Mixed deciduous woodland.

Note the steeply ascending branches and flaky bark in the photo opposite.

Southern Nettle Tree

Celtis australis

(Elm Family)

Shape: Deciduous tree to about 25 m tall.

Leaves: Alternate, arranged in two rows. Stalk 0.5-1.8 cm long; blade 5-16 cm long, lanceolate, with long twisted point. Base asymmetric, margin coarsely toothed. Upper side of leaf dark green and rough, underside grey-green, usually softly hairy.

Flowers: May, with the leaves, hermaphrodite and solitary in the leaf axils, small, long-stalked, with 2 long feathery stigmas. Male flowers also occur, in small clusters.

Fruit: Aug-Oct, a rounded drupe about 1 cm across, growing on a long thin stalk from the leaf axils. Yellow-green at first, later turning red or dark violet. Flesh tasty.

Bark: Beech-like, grey and smooth, becoming flaky with age.

Distribution: S Europe, as far N as S Alps, N Africa, SW Asia. Rarely planted in BI.

Habitat: Sub-mediterranean and Mediterranean broadleaved woods and rocky scrub communities. Wide tolerance; warmth-loving, only found in very mild sites towards the north of its range.

Southern Nettle Tree: leaves

Southern Nettle Tree: leaf, showing long point

White Mulberry ☞

Morus alba

(Mulberry Family)

Shape: Round-crowned deciduous tree to 15 m tall; often a shrub.
Leaves: Alternate. Stalk more than 1.5 cm long and with milky sap. Blade variable in shape, thin, broadly-ovate, pointed and 6-15 cm long. Base of leaf rounded or weakly heart-shaped. Leaf may be simple or with 3-5 lobes; leaf margin with rough teeth. Both leaf surfaces relatively hairless.
Flowers: May-Jun, plant monoecious or dioecious. Male flowers in stalked, pale green catkins 1.5-3 cm long. Female flowers in stalked flowerheads 5-12 mm across, the stalk as long or longer than inflorescence.
Fruit: From Jul, a blackberry-like cluster of drupes, 1-2.5 cm long, stalked. These fruits are pale at first, ripening to pink or purple; edible.
Bark: Photo p. 250.
Distribution: C and E Asia. Common in S and SE Europe and also grown occasionally in C Europe. Rare in BI; grown in a few collections, mainly in England and S Scotland.
Habitat: Scrub, gardens, streets.
Similar species: Black Mulberry.

White Mulberry: fruits of varying ripeness

White Mulberry: the leaves vary in shape; they are longer stalked than those of Black Mulberry

Black Mulberry ❀
Common Mulberry

Morus nigra

(Mulberry Family)

Differs from White Mulberry in the following ways:
Leaves: Shorter stalks and rougher blade, usually clearly heart-shaped at the base. Upper surface of leaf rough, softly hairy beneath.
Flowers: Female inflorescences sessile or short-stalked.
Fruit: Mulberries sessile or short-stalked: ripening to pink or shiny black; edible and tasty.
Distribution: Near East. Widely cultivated in Europe, particularly in wine growing regions. Occasionally naturalized. In BI planted in parks and gardens, mainly in S England.
Note: Mulberry species are ancient plants of cultivation. The leaves provide food for silkworm caterpillars. Black Mulberry is mainly planted for its edible fruit.

Black Mulberry: leaf is markedly heart-shaped at the base (l); fruits unstalked or short stalked (r), unlike those of White Mulberry

Fig ⚘
(Mulberry Family)

Ficus carica

Shape: A short-trunked deciduous tree with a rounded, open crown growing to about 10 m tall; often a shrub. Leaves alternate. Leaf stalk 4-8 cm long; blade thick and leathery, 8-20 cm long and about the same width. Leaf deeply palmately lobed, with 3-5(7) lobes, sometimes unlobed. Heart-shaped at base.

Flowers: The wild form of this species is monoecious, but cultivated forms are dioecious. Individual flowers small, developing inside the pear-shaped fleshy receptacle. Female flowers at the base of the receptacle, male flowers towards the narrow opening at the top (see note).

Fruit: The familiar fig is a pear-shaped fleshy fruit, 5-8 cm long, green, brown or brownish-violet. The ripe flesh which is green or red and tasty, contains the tiny seeds.

Bark: Pale grey, smooth.

Distribution: Mediterranean Region N to S Alps, Turkey, W Asia. Widely cultivated in areas with a similar climate throughout the world. In BI introduced and naturalized in some areas in S.

Habitat: Dry rocky slopes, maquis, alongside stone walls. Frost-sensitive, growing well only in the wine-growing regions in C Europe.

Note: There are two types of cultivated Fig. Trees with fertile female flowers which produce edible figs, and trees with both male and female flowers, which are mainly cultivated to ensure the supply of the Fig Gallwasp (*Blastophaga psenes*). These types of Fig can only develop ripe fruit when grown close to the fertile forms. Most more recent cultivars, however, are able to develop fruit without pollination. Wild Figs, on the other hand, carry three different stages of inflorescence on the same tree. The summer generation develops into ripe figs, the spring generation produces pollen; both ensure the successful reproduction of the Fig Gallwasp.

The photographs opposite show trunk with smooth, grey bark and fruiting branch (above) and planted Fig tree, showing broad crown and short trunk (below).

Ripening figs

Leaves

Fruiting shoots

Northern Japanese Magnolia ✿ ☞
(Magnolia Family)   *Magnolia kobus*

Shape: Broad-crowned deciduous tree growing to 20 m; often a shrub.
Leaves: Alternate, elliptic to obovate, 6-16 cm long, widest at or above the middle, and with a short point. Margins entire.
Flowers: Apr-May, before the leaves, upright, hermaphrodite flowers spreading to 12 cm when open. 6-9 perianth segments, white, sometimes flushed pink at base. 3 smaller petal-like sepals which fall away early.
Fruit: Curved clusters of follicles, about 12 cm long, splitting open when ripe to reveal the seeds.
Distribution: Japan. In Europe grown as a decorative tree in parks and gardens. In BI occasionally planted, especially in S England and Ireland.
Habitat: Wide tolerance. Hardy.
Similar species: Saucer Magnolia.

Northern Japanese Magnolia: leaves and young fruiting head

Northern Japanese Magnolia: open flowers

Saucer Magnolia ✿ ☞
(Magnolia Family)   *Magnolia x soulangiana*

Shape: Shrub or small tree to 6 m tall.
Leaves: Alternate, elliptical to obovate, 10-20 cm long, widest towards short pointed tip, and with entire margins.
Flowers: Apr-Jun, before, with, or after leaves open, upright, tulip-shaped hermaphrodite flowers. Perianth segments (calyx, and corolla similar) white, more or less pink inside, 5-15 cm long.
Fruit: Like those of Northern Japanese Magnolia. *Bark:* Photo p. 250.
Distribution: Garden origin. One of the commonest cultivated forms.
Habitat: Tolerates a wide range of conditions. Hardy.
Similar species: Northern Japanese Magnolia.

Saucer Magnolia: shoot

Saucer Magnolia: tulip-like flowers

Evergreen Magnolia 🌸 ☞
Bull Bay

Magnolia grandiflora

(Magnolia Family)

Shape: Evergreen broadleaved tree, with wide conical crown, growing to about 25 m.

Leaves: Alternate, Eucalyptus-like and very leathery, elliptic to conical, 12-25 cm long, blunt or with short point. Bright shiny dark green and hairless above, covered with rust-brown felty hairs and obvious midrib below.

Flowers: May-Aug, large, erect, sweetly-scented hermaphrodite flowers opening to 15-25 cm wide. The 6-12 perianth segments are pure white, with 3 petal-like sepals.

Fruit: An oval cluster of felty follicles to about 12 cm long. These spring open when ripe to reveal the seeds.

Distribution: SE North America, commonly planted as a decorative tree in Europe. Often grown against walls in BI.

Habitat: Native habitat on damp or wet soils near rivers and marshes. Grows best in the milder parts of Europe.

Evergreen Magnolia: thick, leathery, shiny leaves

Evergreen Magnolia: flower (l); fruiting head (r)

Umbrella Tree 🌸

Magnolia tripetala

(Magnolia Family)

Shape: Broad-crowned deciduous tree to 12 m tall.

Leaves: Alternate, arranged in large whorls at the ends of the shoots (hence common name). 25-60 cm long, elliptic to obovate, pale green.

Flowers: Jun-Jul; after the leaves, large, erect, hermaphrodite flowers about 20 cm across and with a rather unpleasant smell. 6-9 long, white perianth segments, and 3 shorter, greenish, petal-like sepals.

Fruit: Cone-shaped pink clusters of follicles to about 12 cm long. These spring open when ripe to reveal the red seeds.

Distribution: SE North America. In Europe grown as a decorative tree.

Habitat: Damp, rich soils; hardy.

Umbrella Tree: flower surrounded by whorl of spreading leaves

Tulip Tree ✿

(Magnolia Family)

Liriodendron tulipifera

Shape: Fast-growing, straight-trunked, deciduous tree reaching 60 m in its native habitat, and about 35 m in Europe. Crown conical at first, later becoming rounded.

Leaves: Alternate. Leaf stalk about the same length as blade. Blade very variable in shape and more or less rectangular in outline, 8-10 cm long, usually with a 2-lobed tip and 2 lateral lobes. The division between the 2 end lobes forms a wide v-shape. Leaf shiny-green above, somewhat paler and often bluish-green beneath. Autumn colouring golden yellow.

Flowers: May-Jul; after the leaves, large terminal, tulip-like hermaphrodite flowers. Perianth with 3 greenish sepal-like segments, and 6 petal-like segments. The latter are yellow-green or sulphur-yellow with orange speckles towards the base. Stamens numerous and as long as perianth. The numerous carpels are arranged on a spindle-like axis.

Fruit: Oct, upright, brown, conical cluster, 6-8 cm long.

Bark: Dark grey, with longitudinal furrows (photo p. 250).

Distribution: E North America. Popular park and garden tree in Europe, and sometimes planted as an experimental forestry species. In BI frequent in parks and gardens, mainly in S England.

Habitat: Mixed deciduous woodland. Prefers deep, open, damp to moist, rich loamy soils. Dislikes very dry or water-logged conditions. Hardy.

Flowers

Shoot with tulip-like flower

Leaf (l); fruiting head (r)

Cherry Laurel 🏵 ☞ (below)   *Prunus laurocerasus*
(Rose Family)

Shape: Evergreen shrub growing to about 8 m tall, sometimes forming a tree.
Leaves: Alternate, leathery, narrowly elliptical, 5-15(20) cm long. Margins entire or shallowly toothed, edges of leaves rolled under. Leaves shiny dark green and hairless above. Poisonous (contains cyanide).
Flowers: Apr-May, white hermaphrodite flowers to about 1 cm across, in upright racemes 7-15 cm tall.
Fruit: Aug, oval or rounded berries, green, becoming red or black when ripe.
Distribution: SE Europe, Turkey. Often planted in the milder parts of Europe, commonly grown in BI and widely naturalized.
Habitat: Shady, humus-rich sites, often growing as an undershrub. Frost-sensitive.
Similar species: Portugal Laurel (*Prunus lusitanica*) is a native of SW France, Portugal and Spain. Its smaller leaves have slender, dark red stalks.

Strawberry Tree ❋ 🏵 ☞ (above)   *Arbutus unedo*
(Heather Family)

Shape: Evergreen shrub or small tree to about 10 m tall.
Leaves: Alternate, leathery, narrowly elliptical, 10-14 cm long, toothed. Leaves hairless and shiny on both sides.
Flowers: Sep-Dec, hermaphrodite, borne in drooping clusters. Perianth urn-shaped, white to pink.
Fruit: Sep-Dec, strawberry-like, warty, red berries, 1.5-2 cm across (edible).
Bark: Photo p. 251.
Distribution: Mediterranean region, also along the Atlantic coast of Europe as far N as SW Ireland. In BI planted in parks and gardens, especially in S England and Ireland.
Habitat: Rocky scrub and thickets. Frost-sensitive.

Sweet Bay 🏵
Bay Laurel   *Laurus nobilis*
(Laurel Family).

Shape: Evergreen shrub or small tree to about 15 m tall.
Leaves: Alternate, narrowly elliptical, 5-11 cm long, usually with entire, somewhat wavy margins. Strongly aromatic when crushed (used as a herb in cooking).
Flowers: Mar-May, plant dioecious. Flowers in small pale yellow clusters. Male flowers have bright yellow anthers.
Fruit: Shiny reddish-black berries.
Distribution: Mediterranean region. In BI planted and naturalized in some areas, notably SW England and Wales and SW Ireland.
Habitat: Maquis and scrub. Often planted in gardens as an ornamental plant or herb. Frost-sensitive.

Shoot of Strawberry Tree (l) and Sweet Bay (r)

London Plane ⚘

Platanus x hispanica

(Plane Family)

Shape: Deciduous tree growing to about 35 m tall, with heavily branched crown.

Leaves: Maple-like but alternate. Leaf stalk 4-10 cm long. Blade 12-25 cm long and wide, with 3-5(7) pointed lobes. Lobes usually have large teeth. Leaves vary considerably in the depth of the lobing.

Flowers: May; with the leaves, small and inconspicuous. Male and female flowers borne in separate, small, globular clusters on the same tree. Clusters about 1 cm across.

Fruit: Sep-Oct, in dense, round, hairy clusters, 2-3 cm across. These hang individually or in pairs (rarely in 3s) on a long stalk.

Bark: Young bark grey or yellow-brown, becoming flaky and revealing paler patches beneath (photo p. 251).

Distribution: Origin unknown. Widely planted in parks, gardens and along roads. In BI commonest in S, including streets and parks of London.

Habitat: Grows best on moist, deep soils. Deeply-rooting, hardy, light-loving species. Grows well even in relatively polluted urban sites.

Note: London Plane is a hybrid between the American Plane (*P. occidentalis*) and the Oriental Plane (*P. orientalis*). It is sometimes difficult to distinguish it from the latter, which is a native of SE Europe and Turkey. Oriental Plane tends to have leaves with 5-7 narrow lobes and flowers and fruits in clusters of 3 or more.

The photographs opposite show London Plane with broad crown (above) and characteristically patterned flaky bark (below).

Twigs with globular fruit clusters

Leaves (maple-like)

Round clusters of flowers (l), and fruits (r)

Common Hawthorn ❋ 🌣 🖎

(Rose Family)   *Crataegus monogyna*

Shape: Shrub or small tree growing to 10 m tall.

Shoot: Short shoots often specialized as thorns.

Leaves: Alternate, broadly oval or diamond shaped, 3-6 cm long, with 3-7 deep, pointed lobes.

Flowers: May-Jun, in upright terminal clusters. Individual flowers hermaphrodite, 8-15 mm across, 5-partite, usually with a single (rarely 2), style.

Fruit: Sep-Oct, shiny red, rounded, about 1 cm across; each fruit containing a single stone.

Bark: Photo p. 251.

Distribution: Europe, N Africa, Turkey, Caucasus.

Habitat: From lowlands to montane levels. Often at forest edges or along footpaths and in scrub. Prefers dry to moist, mainly calcareous clay or loam. Deep-rooting, light-loving or semi-shade species.

Similar species: Midland Hawthorn.

Common Hawthorn: flowers   Common Hawthorn: leaves with deep lobes

Midland Hawthorn ❋ 🌣 🖎

(Rose Family)   *Crataegus laevigata*

Differs from Common Hawthorn in the following ways:

Leaves: Less deeply cut, with 3(5) more or less blunt lobes.

Flowers: About 2 weeks earlier, Mostly with 2 styles (more rarely 1 or 3).

Fruit: Mostly 2-stoned.

Distribution: Europe; in BI only in lowland England.

Habitat: Moist or damp soils.

Notes: 1) Paul's Scarlet is a pink-flowered garden variety of this species, see photograph opposite (below). 2) Hybrids between Common and Midland Hawthorn are quite common.

Midland Hawthorn: fruits   Midland Hawthorn: leaf

Quince 🌸☞

Cydonia oblonga

(Rose Family)

Shape: Shrub or small tree to 8 m tall.

Leaves: Alternate. Stalk 1-2 cm long, with felty hairs; blade ovate to broadly elliptic, 5-10 cm long, with entire margins, and felty grey hairs below..

Flowers: May-Jun, solitary, hermaphrodite. Petals white or pink, longer than sepals. The photograph opposite (above) shows tree in full flower.

Fruit: Sep-Oct, apple- or pear-shaped, yellow and softly hairy; aromatic smell.

Bark: Photo p. 251.

Distribution: SW Asia. Cultivated in Europe, especially in C and S, sometimes naturalized. Planted in BI and sometimes found in hedges and woods, mainly in the S.

Habitat: Sunny slopes, woodland margins. Warmth-loving, frost-sensitive. Prefers deep, moist, basic soils.

Quince: upper (l) and lower (r) side of leaf

Quince: young fruit showing hairy surface

Medlar 🌸☞

Mespilus germanica

(Rose Family)

Shape: Shrub or small tree to 6 m tall, often thorny.

Leaves: Alternate, very short-stalked. Blade narrowly elliptic to lanceolate, 6-13 cm long, with finely toothed or entire margin; felty beneath..

Flowers: May-Jun, solitary, hermaphrodite, with a long, pointed bract at the base. Petals white, usually shorter than sepals.

Fruit: Oct-Nov, large (2-3 cm across), hard, brown and rounded; flat-topped and crowned by ring of persistent sepals.

Distribution: SW Asia, SE Europe. Planted in S,W and C Europe, sometimes naturalized. In BI planted mainly in S Britain.

Habitat: Sunny slopes, woodland margins, often in wine-growing regions, on base-rich soils.

The photograph opposite (below) shows Medlar fruits.

Medlar: flowering branch

Wild Pear ✤

Pyrus pyraster

(Rose Family)

Shape: Medium-sized densely branching broadleaved tree, to 20 m tall.

Shoot: Short shoots often modified as thorns.

Leaves: Alternate, stalk as long or longer than blade. Blade oval or rounded, 2-8 cm long, and finely toothed. Hairy on both sides at first, but soon losing hairs; shiny dark green above.

Flowers: Apr-May, often before leaves are fully out, in clusters of 3-9, hermaphrodite, 2-4 cm across, with 5 white (rarely pink) petals and felty calyx; many stamens, anthers red; 5 separate styles (unlike Apple).

Fruit: Sep-Oct, pear-shaped or rounded, 2-3 cm across, brownish-yellow. Flesh has many gritty stone-cells, and a sharp taste.

Bark: Grey-brown, cracking into small plates (photo p. 251).

Distribution: Europe, W Asia. In BI scattered, mainly towards S and C.

Habitat: Lowland to montane levels (in Alps to 850 m); mixed deciduous woods (e.g. oak-elm valley woods, and mixed oak woods), hedges, scrub. Damp to dry, rich, basic, mainly calcareous soils in sites with warm summers. Deep-rooting light-loving or semi-shade species.

Note: Common Pear ✤ (*Pyrus communis*) is closely related and of garden origin; it exists in many different varieties, and is also found in the wild. Most cultivated forms of this species have larger, softer, sweeter fruits, and are usually thornless. It is often difficult to distinguish some forms of wild Common Pear from the true Wild Pear. Wild Pears may often originate from the stock used in former orchards or gardens.

Flowers, showing red anthers

Fruits

Wild Pear: thorn (l); rounded leaf (r)

Crab Apple * ⊛
(Rose Family)

Malus sylvestris

Shape: Deciduous tree to 10 m tall, with densely branching, rounded crown. Twigs often with short thorns.

Leaves: Alternate. Stalk 1.5-4 cm long; blade broadly elliptical, or rounded oval, with short point, 3-8 cm long, simply or doubly toothed, and rounded or weakly heart-shaped at base. Hairy at first, becoming smooth, but retaining hairs on vein axils beneath.

Flowers: Apr-May; with the leaves, at ends of short shoots in few-flowered clusters. Stalk short, hairless or slightly hairy. 5 petals, each 1-2 cm long, white on inside, pink outside; sepals small, with felty lining. Anthers yellow. Usually 5 styles, fused at base.

Fruit: Sep-Oct, small, round apples, 2-3 cm across, yellow-green, flushed red when ripe; dry and sour to taste.

Bark: Grey-brown, cracking into small plates.

Distribution: Most of Europe, W Asia. In BI throughout, except far N.

Habitat: Lowlands, montane levels (rarely above 1100 m in the Alps). Mixed deciduous woods, river valley woods, wood margins, hedgerows, scrub. Deep, moist, fertile, base-rich soils. Shallow-rooting light-loving or semi-shade species.

Note: Crab Apple is one of the parent species used in the development of the Cultivated Apple (*Malus domestica*). The Cultivated Apple is thornless, the leaves are hairier beneath, the flower stalks felty, and the fruits bigger and sweeter. This species is often naturalized and in BI is commoner than Crab Apple. Wild forms often have small, sour fruits. Commercial orchards now use only a fraction of the original range of cultivars.

The photographs opposite show Cultivated Apple in full flower (above) and in fruit (below).

Fruits often stay on the tree after the leaves have fallen

Flowers

Leaf: upper side (l); lower side (r)

Swedish Whitebeam *⊛☞   *Sorbus intermedia*
(Rose Family)

Shape: Deciduous tree to 15 m tall, with oval or conical crown.
Leaves: Alternate. Stalk 1-3 cm long; blade broadly elliptic, 6-11 cm long,
the lobes deepening towards the base. Leaves irregularly toothed, shiny
above, grey and with felty hairs beneath, becoming hairless.
Flowers: May-June, in many-flowered clusters; white.
Fruit: Sep-Oct, thick clusters of round or oval berries, 1-1.3 cm across,
orange-red when ripe.

Distribution: N Europe. The true
Swedish Whitebeam is found
scattered in BI. It is introduced, but
also spreads naturally.
Habitat: Deciduous woods, damp,
rocky sites.
Similar species: Common
Whitebeam (p. 220).
Note: There are several native variants
related to Swedish Whitebeam in the
BI. They are mainly endemic to rocky
sites in the W.

Swedish Whitebeam: upper (l) and lower (r)
leaf surface

Note: Sorbus x thuringiaca, a hybrid
of Rowan *S. aucuparia* (p. 84) and *S. aria* (p. 220), has leaves resembling
those of *S. intermedia* but with one or two pairs of free leaflets at the
base. It is commonly planted in the BI, in parks and gardens, and along
streets, especially in the fastigiate (tall and narrow) variant. It sometimes
appears naturally, where both parents occur together.

Wild Service Tree *⊛   *Sorbus torminalis*
(Rose Family)

Shape: Deciduous tree to 22 m tall, with oval crown.
Leaves: Alternate. Stalk 2-5 cm long, thin; blade broadly oval, 6-12 cm
long and wide, with 3-4(5) toothed, pointed, unequal lobes. Shiny green
above, paler below. Leaves turn yellow, red or purple in autumn.
Flowers: May-Jun, after the leaves, upright, flattened clusters. Individual
flowers hermaphrodite, 1-1.5 cm across.
Fruit: Sep-Oct, round or oval berries, each about 1.5 cm long; yellow-red,
ripening to brown with pale spots.
Bark: Grey and smooth, becoming dark brown and flaky (photo p. 251).

Distribution: S, W and C Europe,
W Asia, N Africa. In BI native and
local in England and Wales.
Habitat: Lowlands up to about 750
m; rather local in mixed oak woods
and scrub. Prefers dry or damp,
base-rich soils, but does also grow in
slightly acid conditions.
Warmth-loving, relatively
deep-rooted semi-shade species.

Wild Service Tree: leaf (l), showing pointed
lobes; flower cluster (r)

Common Whitebeam * ✿ ✾

(Rose Family)

Sorbus aria

Shape: Small deciduous tree to 15 m tall, with oval or rounded crown. Often a shrub with erect branches.

Shoot: Covered in grey felty hairs at first, becoming hairless, reddish olive brown.

Leaves: Alternate. Stalk 1-2 cm long, with soft, white hairs; blade broadly elliptic, 6-12 cm long, unevenly toothed. Dark green and shiny above, white felty hairs beneath.

Flowers: May-Jun, after the leaves, in terminal many-flowered clusters, hermaphrodite, 5-partite. Flower-stalk and calyx hairy. Petals white, 3-4 mm long, calyx much shorter. 2, rarely 3, styles.

Fruit: Sep-Oct, thickly clustered round or oval berries, each 1-1.5 cm across, mostly with 2 seeds and ripening scarlet. Remain on tree through the winter.

Bark: Grey, smooth, usually with irregular marbling, developing cracks with age (photo p. 251).

Distribution: Most of Europe, N Africa, Turkey. In BI native but rather local, and commonly planted.

Habitat: Lowland to subalpine zone (Alps to 1600 m); sunny rocky sites, scrub, oak, beech and pine woods. Basic or slightly acid soils. Hardy, deep-rooting light-loving or semi-shade species. Decorative tree in parks and gardens..

Similar species: Swedish Whitebeam (p. 218).

Note: There are several native variants related to Common Whitebeam in the British Isles. They are mainly endemic to rocky sites in the W.

The photographs opposite show Common Whitebeam shrub in native habitat (above) and a small planted tree (below).

Twig with unripe fruit

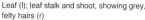

Leaf (l); leaf stalk and shoot, showing grey, felty hairs (r)

Clustered flowers

Bright red fruits

Wild Cherry * ✿
Gean

Prunus avium

(Rose Family)

Shape: Deciduous tree to 20(30) m tall. Short-trunked with rounded crown when growing in the open; with tall, unbranched trunk and high crown when growing in closed woodland.

Leaves: Alternate, rather thin and limp. Stalk 2-5 cm long, with 2 red glands; blade obovate to elliptic, pointed, 7-15 cm long, toothed; hairless above, hairy on veins below. Turning red or yellow in autumn.

Flowers: Apr-May, just before the leaves appear, clustered in groups of 2-6, on previous season's shoots. Hermaphrodite, long-stalked, 5-partite. Petals white, 1-1.5 cm long; sepals turned back.

Fruit: Jul, round cherries, 1-1.5 cm across, ripening to a glossy black-red, with large pale stone. The flesh of the wild form is bitter-sweet.

Bark: Smooth at first, shiny grey- or reddish-brown, with horizontal peeling bands (photo p. 251).

Distribution: Europe, W Siberia, Turkey, Caucasus, N Africa. In BI native and found throughout. Also planted in parks and gardens.

Habitat: Lowland and mountains (Alps to 1700 m); broadleaved woods, wood margins, hedgerows. Usually on calcareous loam soils. Not deep-rooting, light-loving or semi-shade species.

Notes: 1) Cultivated cherries are derived from this wild species.
2) Dwarf Cherry, *P. cerasus*, native of SW Asia, is a widespread introduction. Differences from Wild Cherry include: leaves smaller, stiffer and shiny; stalk with or without glands; flower stalk shorter; fruit bright red and sour.

The photographs opposite show Wild Cherry in spring (above) and autumn (below).

Flowering twig

Leaf (l); leaf stalk showing 2 red glands (r)   Cluster of flowers

Cherry Plum 🌸

(Rose Family)

Prunus cerasifera

Shape: Spreading, open-crowned broadleaved tree to about 8 m tall.
Leaves: Oval or elliptic, to 6 cm long and 3 cm across, with toothed margins. Dark glossy green above, paler and downy on veins beneath.
Flowers: Mar-Apr, appear before leaves. White, to 2.5 cm across, with 5 petals, singly or in small clusters.
Fruit: Jun-Aug, pale green, round, plum-like, ripening to red. Rarely fruits in BI.
Bark: Purple-brown, scaly, with orange horizontal lenticels (photo p. 251).
Distribution: Balkans, C Asia. Introduced to BI and widely planted along streets, in hedges and gardens, especially as purplish-leaved form (*P. cerasifera* var. *pissardii*).

Cherry Plum: flowering twig

Bird Cherry ✿ 🌸 ☞

(Rose Family)

Prunus padus

Shape: Deciduous tree to about 18 m tall, often multi-trunked, with overhanging branches.
Shoot: Damaged bark has an unpleasant smell.
Leaves: Alternate. Stalk 1-2 cm long, with 1-2 glands; blade elliptic, pointed, 6-12 cm long, finely toothed, matt green above, blue-green below, lateral veins curving and joining together towards margin.
Flowers: May-June, appearing after leaf growth. White, 5-partite, hermaphrodite and fragrant, in dense drooping racemes 10-15 cm long.
Fruit: Jul-Aug, pea-sized rounded berry, glossy black when ripe; stone furrowed; flesh bitter.
Bark: Smooth, dark grey, occasionally with shallow cracks (photo p. 251).
Distribution: Europe, much of Asia. In BI native and also much planted.
Habitat: River valleys, in mountains to 1800 m; damp broadleaved woods, wet woods and scrub, woodland edges, and near water. Deep, damp, rich, basic loamy or clay soils. Semi-shade species; suckering. Decorative tree.

Bird Cherry: flowering shoots

Bird Cherry: twig with young fruits (l); leaf showing lateral veins joining towards the margin (r)

Judas Tree ⊛

Cercis siliquastrum

(Pea Family)

Shape: Small, open, many-branched deciduous tree, to 10 m tall.

Leaves: Alternate. Stalk 2-4 cm long; blade circular or kidney-shaped, 8-12 cm across, with heart-shaped base, hairless both sides, and with entire margin.

Flowers: Mar-May, before leaves, pink, stalked, hermaphrodite, about 2 cm across, each shaped like pea flower, and with 10 unfused stamens. Clustered along older twigs, branches and even on trunk.

Fruit: Sep-Oct, pods, 7-10 cm long, flat, with pointed tip, green at first, turning pink or red to dark brown, with parchment-like texture when ripe. Pods remain on tree until spring.

Bark: Smooth and red or olive-brown at first, becoming grey-brown and cracking with age (photo p. 251).

Distribution: Native to E Mediterranean; now spread throughout Mediterranean (as far N as S Alps) and W Asia. In BI often grown in gardens and parks, mainly in S England.

Habitat: Open broadleaved woods and scrub, often with Downy Oak and Hop Hornbeam, river beds, rocky sites; usually on calcareous soils. Warmth- and light-loving species. Often planted in streets or gardens. Only hardy in milder parts of Europe.

Kidney-shaped leaves

The flowers appear just before the leaves

Flowers on trunk (l); pods (r)

Orange ☞

(Rue Family)

Citrus sinensis

Shape: Evergreen broadleaved tree to 13 m tall, with rounded crown and green, often thorny, stems.

Leaves: Alternate, with narrowly winged stalk. Blade shiny dark green, leathery, elliptic, pointed.

Flowers: Feb-June, in leaf axils, solitary or in small groups; each 2-3 cm across, white and sweetly scented.

Fruit: Mainly Dec-Apr, the familiar orange, usually orange in colour but sometimes yellow or green; flesh sweet.

Distribution: China. Cultivated in Mediterranean region and in many parts of the world with a suitable climate (e.g. parts of USA, Japan, Brazil). Cannot be grown outside in BI.

Habitat: Needs warm, subtropical climate on loose, well-drained soil.

Orange: evergreen, shiny leaves and creamy-white flowers

Orange: shoots (l); fruits (r)

Lemon ☞

(Rue Family)

Citrus limon

Shape: Evergreen broadleaved tree to 7m tall, with rounded crown. Twigs have up to 3 long spines.

Leaves: Alternate. Stalk scarcely winged; blade leathery, elliptic, pointed, finely toothed, shiny dark green above.

Flowers: All year, like those of Orange, but somewhat smaller, white, often suffused pink.

Fruit: Mainly Dec-Apr, the familiar lemon, 7-15 cm long, rough; flesh sour.

Distribution: Asia. Grown in Mediterranean region and many subtropical countries. Cannot be grown outside in BI.

Habitat: As for Orange.

Lemon; young fruits

Lemon: ripe fruit

Holly *⊛
(Holly Family)

Ilex aquifolium

Shape: Evergreen shrub or small tree, to 10 m tall, with conical crown, but very variable in shape, especially the many garden varieties.

Leaves: Alternate. Stalk 5-15 mm long; blade stiff and leathery, oval to elliptic, pointed, 3-9 cm long and about half as wide. Margin very variable: usually with sharp spines, but often entire (even on the same plant), with all possible intermediates. Smooth on both sides, shiny dark green above, paler below.

Flowers: May-Jun, tree dioecious. Flowers clustered in the axils of leaves; white, with pinkish base, small, mostly 4-partite. Female flowers show prominent green ovary.

Fruit: Sep-Oct, round berry, 7-10 mm across, shiny red when ripe, containing 4 (rarely 5) seeds. Fruits often stay on tree over the winter or even longer and provide a good source of food for birds (particularly thrushes).

Bark: Smooth, thin and silvery or dark grey (photo p. 251).

Distribution: W, C and S Europe, N Africa, W Asia, China. In BI native throughout, and often planted.

Habitat: Mainly in areas with oceanic climate, in lowland and into mountains (Alps to 1800 m). Sometimes forms undergrowth in woods, especially Beech, woodland margins, scrub. Likes moist, fairly rich soils. Suckering; shade species. Often planted as decorative tree in gardens and as a hedge. There are many cultivated forms, some with variegated leaves, some virtually spineless. Photograph opposite shows the garden variety 'Pyramidalis'.

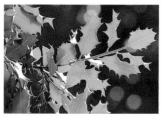

Twig with leathery, evergreen leaves

Twig with clusters of flowers in leaf axils (l); berries (r)

Leaves, showing variation in shape

Leaves, showing variation in shape

Small-leaved Lime * ✲

Tilia cordata

(Lime Family)

Shape: Deciduous tree to 38 m tall. Has relatively short trunk and wide, low, dense, evenly domed crown when growing in the open, but a tall, unbranched trunk and high crown when growing in closed stands.

Shoot: Finely hairy at first, quickly becoming smooth and shiny.

Leaves: Alternate, arranged in 2 rows. Stalk 2-5 cm long, hairless. Blade heart-shaped, 3-10 cm long (smaller than those of Large-leaved Lime), pointed, with finely- and sharply-toothed margin. Hairless, except for vein axils on grey-green lower surface, which have brownish hairs.

Flowers: Jun-Jul, after the leaves, 4-11 yellow-white, strongly scented hermaphrodite flowers, grouped in hanging clusters; stalk fused with a pale green, tongue-shaped bract; perianth 5-partite.

Fruit: Sep, rounded, 5-8 mm across (smaller than those of Large-leaved Lime), woody, grey-green, single-seeded; not obviously ribbed. Fruits fall from tree with the wing-like bract when ripe.

Bark: Smooth and thin at first, later becoming dark grey or blackish, with longitudinal ridges (photo p. 251).

Distribution: Europe, W Siberia, Asia. Native in C England (N to Lake District) and Wales; also planted, and naturalized.

Habitat: Lowland to montane levels (Alps to 1400 m). Mixed broadleaved woods (oak–Hornbeam woods, river–valley woods). Moist or slightly dry, open, base-rich loamy soils. In Britain especially on limestone cliffs. Late frost-sensitive, deeply-rooting shade species; sensitive to air pollution. Commonly planted in parks and along streets.

Similar species: Large-leaved Lime, Silver Lime (p. 234).

The photographs opposite show Small-leaved Lime in spring (above) and summer (below).

Upper (l) and lower (r) sides of leaf. Note brownish hairs on vein axils on underside

Flowering shoot

Small-leaved Lime has smaller, more numerous fruits than Large-leaved Lime

Large-leaved Lime * ✿ ☞

Tilia platyphyllos

(Lime Family)

Shape: Deciduous tree to 34 m tall.

Leaves: Stalk softly hairy; blade to 17 cm long (often larger still on vigorous shoots), usually softly hairy on both sides, especially on vein axils.

Flowers: Jun, 1-2 weeks before Small-leaved Lime. Flowers somewhat larger; inflorescence with 2-5 flowers.

Fruit: Sep, 8-10 mm long, hard, with obvious ribs.

Bark: Dark grey, finely ridged.

Distribution: C, W, S Europe, Turkey, Caucasus. Native in England and Wales, but very local as wild species, e.g. Wye Valley and S Yorkshire; more common as introduction.

Habitat: Mixed broadleaved woodland, especially in hills and mountains, in sites with warm summers, mild winters and high air humidity. Moist, fertile, base-rich soils.

Similar species: Small-leaved Lime (p. 232), Silver Lime.

Note: The lime most often seen planted in parks and gardens is the Common Lime, *Tilia* x *europaea*. This is a hybrid between Small-leaved and Large-leaved Limes. The hairs on the undersides of its leaves are restricted to the vein axils. The tree (and ground beneath) is often covered with sticky honeydew in summer, from the aphids which find this species very attractive.

Large-leaved Lime: leaf (l); fruits are in small groups (r)

Silver Lime ✿ ☞

Tilia tomentosa

(Lime Family)

Shape: Deciduous tree to 30 m tall.

Shoot: With grey felty hairs.

Leaves: Alternate, in two rows. Stalk felty; blade heart-shaped, with grey or white felty hairs beneath. Autumn colour golden yellow.

Flowers: Jul, as for Small-leaved Lime.

Fruit: Sep-Oct, rounded, hard, hairy, rather bumpy and weakly ribbed.

Bark: Grey, with shallow ridges (photo p. 251).

Distribution: SE Europe, Turkey, where found in mixed woodland. In BI occasionally planted, especially in London and other city parks, and in large gardens.

Similar species: Small-leaved Lime (p. 232), Large-leaved Lime.

Silver Lime: upper (l) and lower (r) surface of leaf

Sea Buckthorn *⚘

Hippophae rhamnoides

(Sea Buckthorn Family)

Shape: Much-branched shrub or small tree, to 10 m tall, with thorny twigs.

Shoot: With silvery scales.

Leaves: Alternate. Stalk only 1-3 mm long; blade long and narrow, 2-7 cm long and at most 1 cm wide, with entire margin and mealy on both sides. Dark green above, silvery below.

Flowers: Mar-Apr, before the leaves, plant dioecious. Flowers on previous year's growth. Male flowers yellow-brown, about 3 mm across, stalkless, in rounded clusters; calyx forming a hood over the 4 stamens. Female flowers very inconspicuous; ovary and yellow-green stigma surrounded by greenish calyx tube. Inflorescences often grow in thorn or leaf axils.

Fruit: Sep, juicy, edible (but sour), orange, single-seeded, berry-like, oval, about 6-8 mm long; rich in vitamin C. Important source of food for migrant birds.

Bark: Smooth and dark brown, becoming ridged and grey-brown (photo p. 251).

Distribution: Europe and Asia. In BI possibly native only in E England, but widely planted.

Habitat: In BI mainly coastal (especially dunes). On mainland Europe from the coast to subalpine levels; pioneer scrub on dunes, river gravel, in gravel pits and open pine woods. Dry, flooded sand or gravel; usually calcareous. Deep-rooting, suckering, light-loving species. Decorative garden plant.

Note: Sea Buckthorn absorbs nitrogen via symbiotic root bacteria (Actinomycetes), and thus improves the soil.

♂ flowers (l); ripe fruits (r)

Twig with narrow, silver-haired leaves

Thorny shoot with clusters of ♂ flowers which appear before the leaves

Southern Blue-gum ✿

(Myrtle Family)

Eucalyptus globulus

Shape: Rapidly growing evergreen broadleaved tree, reaching 65 m in native region, about 40 m in Europe. Trunk straight, crown loose, conical at first, later rounded.

Leaves: Two different kinds. Leaves on young shoots are oval, opposite and unstalked, about 8-15 cm long; blue-green and mealy. Leaves on older shoots are alternate, leathery, lanceolate and often curved, 10-30 cm long, stalked, drooping and shiny dark green.

Flowers: Jun-Sep, solitary or in groups of up to 3, in the leaf axils. Flask-shaped mealy flower buds have lid formed by fused petals which falls away to reveal many white or pink stamens.

Fruit: Woody, many-seeded capsule, to 3 cm across.

Bark: Smooth, peeling into long strips to leave a patchwork of white, beige, grey, pink and brown (photo p. 251).

Distribution: SE Australia, Tasmania. Now introduced to many other parts of the world, including Mediterranean and Ireland. In BI planted as ornamental (rarely forestry) tree; self-sown in W Ireland.

Habitat: Undemanding, often used for wet soils in forestry. Planted in parks and along streets. Not hardy.

Notes: 1) The leaves provide eucalyptus oil which is used in many medicines.
2) Several other species have been planted in BI, notably Cider Gum, *E. gunnii*, which is commonest in Ireland and S and W Britain.

Mealy flower buds and open flowers, showing many stamens

Smooth, peeling bark (l); shoot & young leaves (r)

Leaves: oval, opposite, unstalked young leaves (l); alternate, leathery, lanceolate, curved older leaves (r)

Tree Biology

Trees are tall (usually over 5 m), woody plants with a more or less distinct trunk. By contrast, shrubs are usually lower-growing, with several or many stems growing up from the base. However, there are many intermediates between trees and shrubs.

Conifers (*Coniferae*, with about 800 species world-wide) belong to the naked-seeded plants, or gymnosperms (*Gymnospermae*). This group is distinguished by its naked seeds; their seeds are not enclosed in an ovary. Conifers have leaves which are either needle-shaped or scale-like, and they are, with some notable exceptions (e.g. larch, Dawn Redwood, Swamp Cypress) evergreen. *Ginkgo*, although not a true conifer, is a gymnosperm. It has unique fan-shaped leaves.

The **broadleaved trees** are a much larger group, belonging to the angiosperms (*Angiospermae*), or flowering plants, which have seeds enclosed in an ovary. Most of the broadleaved trees in this book are deciduous, but some are evergreen.

Trees, like other seed-plants, consist of the three basic organs: **root**, **shoot** and **leaves**.

The shoot

The shoot system is divided up into **nodes**, from which the leaves emerge, with **internodes** between. In woody plants, the woody tissue develops at the end of each growing season. Side branches grow from the main branch, emerging from buds in the leaf axils. These side branches may themselves branch, resulting in a **shoot system**. Tree shoots become thicker and thicker each season by the process of **secondary thickening**, and these become **twigs** or **branches**. Together these build up to form the **crown** of the tree, whose basic shape is subject to much variation through different environmental influences. In most broadleaved trees the main trunk divides at a certain height into a number of strong branches. In most conifers it continues for the full height of the tree, with side branches growing downwards on either side.

The **bark** of a tree covers the trunk, branches and twigs with a (usually) smooth woody layer. It has wart-like **lenticels** in its surface, and these vary in density and pattern from species to species. The lenticels allow transfer of gases across the bark barrier. Sometimes the cork in the bark projects out from the trunk or twigs, as in the corky wings of Field Maple. As it ages, bark may change its colour, thickness and texture, and such changes are often important identification characters. Some species, such as Common Beech, Hazel and Rowan, retain their smooth, young-looking bark throughout their lives.

The leaf

Leaves are normally flat structures, coloured green by the chlorophyll they contain. Using this pigment, they are able to manufacture their own vital sugars and starch from carbon dioxide in the air and water. In conifers, the leaves are usually reduced to narrow, needle-shaped structures.

Leaves are arranged in particular patterns on the shoot, including:

- three or more leaves at each node, described as **whorled**, or in whorls;

- two leaves, one at each side of the node, termed **opposite**;

- a single leaf at each node, termed **alternate** leaves;

- needles arranged horizontally in a comb-like pattern, known as **spreading**;

- Needles arranged evenly around the twig, termed **radially inserted.**

whorled   opposite   alternate   spreading   radial

Leaf structure

A fully developed leaf consists of the leaf blade, the leafstalk (petiole), and leaf base (see drawing). The **leaf base** is usually no more than an inconspicuous thickening at the bottom of the leafstalk.

Stipules, which grow at the sides of the leaf base, are usually small, and in many trees they fall away early. In some cases, e.g. *Robinia*, the stipules take the form of thorns.

Sometimes the **leafstalk** is very short, or even absent altogether, in which case the leaf is termed **sessile**, or unstalked.

There is much variation in the shape of the leaf blade. If the blade is

lateral vein

blade

midrib

leafstalk

stipule
leafbase

imparipinnate	paripinnate	trifoliate

undivided, the leaf is known as **simple**; **compound** leaves consist of separate leaflets, attached to a common central axis, or **rachis**. When these leaflets are paired along the central stem, the leaves are known as **pinnate**. If there is a **terminal leaflet** (see drawing), the leaf is known as **imparipinnate**; if there is no terminal leaflet, it is **paripinnate**. In **twice pinnate** leaves, the leaflets are themselves divided. If there is just one pair of leaflets in addition to the terminal leaflet, then the leaf is called **trifoliate**.

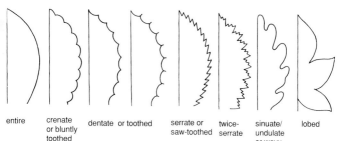

entire	crenate or bluntly toothed	dentate or toothed	serrate or saw-toothed	twice-serrate	sinuate/ undulate or wavy	lobed

There are also differences in leaf **margins**, including (see drawing): The leaf contains **veins** or **nerves** which carry the conductive vessels through the blade. The central vein is called the **midrib**, and this often branches into **lateral veins**.

The flower

The flower is a thickened shoot which carries the reproductive parts of the plant, the individual parts being modified leaves. The fully developed flower (see drawing) consists of the **sepals** (usually green), the **petals** (often attractively coloured), and the central reproductive parts. The sepals and petals are known collectively as **perianth segments**, and in some flowers they are not differentiated into sepals and petals. In such cases one speaks of the **perianth**. The petals make up the **corolla**, and the sepals the **calyx**. Sometimes the petals or sepals may be fused, forming a corolla or calyx tube. The male part of the flower (**androecium**) consists of the **stamens**; the female part (**gynoecium**) consists of the ovary, style and stigma, together known as the **pistil**. The stamens, of which there are usually several, each consist of a thin **filament** and an **anther**, the latter containing the **pollen**. The gynoecium consists of at least one **carpel**, often more, either free or

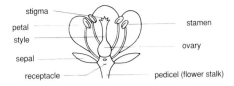

fused. In gymnosperms (including conifers) these are open; in angiosperms (including broadleaved trees) they form a closed structure, the **pistil**, consisting of **ovary**, **style** and **stigma**.

Trees show many variations of the basic flower structure described here. Many tree flowers have reduced perianth segments, or lack them altogether, as an adaptation to wind-pollination (most trees are pollinated by wind). These are sometimes called **naked flowers**.

In many trees, the flowers are of a single sex (**unisexual**), not **hermaphrodite** or **bisexual** (both sexes in the one flower). Male flowers have stamens but no carpels; female flowers carpels but no stamens. An individual tree (or any plant) which has separate male and female flowers (unisexual flowers) is termed **monoecious**; if it carries flowers of one sex only it is termed **dioecious**.

Flowers seldom occur individually on the shoot; usually they are arranged in groups, or **inflorescences**, of which several types are recognized:

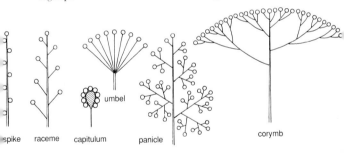

Catkins are (usually) hanging spikes or racemes of inconspicuous flowers which drop off after flowering. In alders and conifers, the female inflorescences become woody as they ripen, forming **cones**. Conifers, however, do not develop fruit. Their cones have the following structure. The central spindle (axis) supports the **cone scales**, which become woody as they ripen. The reproductive scales grow in the axils of protective bracts. In the male cone, the reproductive scales contain the microspores, which develop into winged pollen grains. In the female cone, the reproductive scales contain the ovules. In some genera, such as

Abies and *Pseudotsuga*, the bracts are clearly visible sticking out from between the scales, even on ripe cones. In other genera, such as *Picea*, they are not usually visible on the ripe cones.

The fruit

The fruit develops from the flower as the seeds ripen. In general, the fruit develops after pollination from the ovary, which may consist of one or more carpels. The tissue of the ovary becomes the **pericarp**, which surrounds the seed or seeds.

There are also fruits formed from other parts of the flower, in addition to the ovary, and these are sometimes called false-fruits. Examples are the apple-type (**pome**) fruits of certain members of the rose family. The characteristic feature of such fruits is that the part which encloses the seeds (pip in the case of apple) is itself surrounded by fleshy tissue derived from the flower-shoot. Other common types of fruit are:

- legume: usually long pod, derived from a single carpel, becoming dry when ripe and splitting open from both sides (e.g. *Robinia*);

- capsule: formed from more than one carpel, becoming dry when ripe and usually containing many seeds (e.g. *Paulownia*);

- nut: pericarp becoming hard and thick-walled as it ripens (e.g. *Quercus robur*);

- stone-fruit (drupe): pericarp consisting of an inner, hard, woody stone and an outer part which is either soft and fleshy (e.g. *Prunus*) or leathery (e.g. *Juglans*).

As with flowers, fruits usually develop in a group, or **infructescence**.

Plant naming (nomenclature)

The scientific name of a plant consists of two Latin words. The first denotes the genus, and this, together with the second, forms the species name. This is followed by the name (often in shortened form) of the botanist who first described that species.

Diseases of trees and forests

Those who concern themselves with trees will naturally wish to know something about their illnesses. Some diseases only lessen the attractiveness of the plant, whilst others destroy flowers and fruits, or may even threaten the life of the tree itself.

Diseases also affect trees in their natural forest habitats. In most cases a weakened tree will be quickly overtopped by its neighbours, which may themselves be completely unaffected. On the other hand, if the disease organism is highly infectious and thrives under the particular climate, it may infect many individual trees simultaneously, creating die-back of the forest. In this way entire swathes of forest may be lost or threatened, altering the ecology of the whole region. Examples of this kind of epidemic are those caused by the fungus *Lophodermium seditiosum* and also those transmitted by bark beetles.

Elm disease is a well-known tree disease. The pathogen, *Ceratocystis ulmi*, seems to decimate native populations of *Ulmus glabra* and *U. minor*, on a somewhat cyclic basis. Other examples are the pathogen causing Sweet Chestnut disease (*Endothia parasitica*) and the fungus (*Cronartium ribicola*) which now infects five-needled pines virtually worldwide. The economic losses in the wake of such epidemics are considerable, and successful control methods have yet to be found. However, the diseases are restricted to certain species or groups of related species, and these diseases do not pose a general threat to forests.

Particular problems may arise when fungal or animal pests are introduced to new areas in which the native trees have not been exposed to them before.

In recent years we have been confronted by a disease syndrome which is indeed threatening forests. A general forest die-back has spread in just a few years over large parts of Europe, and more recently in North America and Asia as well, involving all tree species, broadleaved as well as coniferous. The causes and symptoms of this illness have not yet been fully explained, but air pollution certainly seems to be involved. Sulphur dioxide and oxides of nitrogen, from the burning of fossil fuels, often play a key role. They damage leaves and needles, either directly, or indirectly through the effects of acid rain, which acidifies the forest floor by leaching out nutrients and releasing aluminium ions poisonous to plants.

It is worth remembering that, in addition to these much-discussed compounds, the air contains a whole host of other pollutants whose effects on plants, let alone on animals and people, have been at best only insufficiently investigated. The most urgent measure to combat forest die-back is therefore the reduction of pollutants in the air, for example by removing sulphur from emissions from coal-fired power stations and by fitting catalytic convertors to car exhausts.

Bark – Conifers (pages 8–44)

Silver Fir
(p. 8)

Caucasian Fir
(p. 10)

Giant Fir
(p. 12)

Colorado Fir
(p. 14)

Douglas Fir
(p. 18)

Eastern Hemlock
(p. 20)

Western Hemlock
(p. 20)

Norway Spruce
(p. 22)

Serbian Spruce
(p. 26)

Wellingtonia
(p. 30)

Japanese Red
Cedar (p. 30)

Swamp Cypress
(p. 32)

Dawn Redwood
(p. 34)

Yew
(p. 40)

European Larch
(p. 42)

Japanese Larch
(p. 44)

Bark – Conifers (pages 46–76)

Atlas Cedar
(p. 46)

Cedar of Lebanon
(p. 48)

Deodar
(p. 48)

Scots Pine
(p. 50)

Austrian Pine
(p. 54)

Stone Pine
(p. 56)

Maritime Pine
(p. 58)

Aleppo Pine
(p. 58)

Western Yellow
Pine (p. 60)

Weymouth Pine
(p. 64)

Bhutan Pine
(p. 66)

Lawson's Cypress
(p. 70)

Nootka Cypress
(p. 72)

White Cedar
(p. 74)

Western Red Cedar
(p. 76)

Hiba
(p. 76)

Bark – Broadleaved trees (pages 78–112)

Walnut
(p. 78)

Black Walnut
(p. 80)

Caucasian Wingnut
(p. 82)

Tree of Heaven
(p. 82)

Rowan
(p. 84)

True Service Tree
(p. 86)

Common Laburnum
(p. 88)

False Acacia
(p. 90)

Honey Locust
(p. 92)

Horse Chestnut
(p. 98)

Common Ash
(p. 100)

Manna Ash
(p. 102)

Elder
(p. 104)

Sycamore
(p. 106)

Field Maple
(p. 110)

Sugar Maple
(p. 112)

Bark – Broadleaved trees (pages 116–154)

Smooth Japanese Maple (p. 116)

Buckthorn (p. 118)

Paulownia (p. 124)

Ginkgo (p. 128)

Black Poplar (p. 130)

Aspen (p. 134)

Grey Poplar (p. 136)

White Willow (p. 140)

European Violet Willow (p. 146)

Silver Birch (p. 148)

Downy Birch (p. 150)

River Birch (p. 152)

Himalayan Birch (p. 152)

Monarch Birch (p. 154)

Ermans Birch (p. 154)

Chinese Red-barked Birch (p. 154)

Bark – Broadleaved trees (pages 156–204)

Common Alder
(p. 156)

Grey Alder
(p. 158)

Hornbeam
(p. 160)

Hop Hornbeam
(p. 162)

Hazel
(p. 164)

Common Beech
(p. 166)

Sweet Chestnut
(p. 170)

English Oak
(p. 174)

Downy Oak
(p. 176)

Turkey Oak
(p. 178)

Cork Oak
(p. 180)

Red Oak
(p. 184)

European White
Elm (p. 192)

Black Mulberry
(p. 196)

Saucer Magnolia
(p. 200)

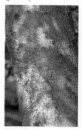
Tulip Tree
(p. 204)

Bark – Broadleaved trees (pages 206–238)

Strawberry Tree
(p. 206)

London Plane
(p. 208)

Common Hawthorn
(p. 210)

Quince
(p. 212)

Wild Pear
(p. 214)

Wild Service Tree
(p. 218)

Common
Whitebeam (p. 220)

Wild Cherry
(p. 222)

Bird Cherry
(p. 224)

Cherry Plum
(p. 224)

Judas Tree
(p. 226)

Holly
(p. 230)

Small Leaved Lime
(p. 232)

Silver Lime
(p. 234)

Sea Buckthorn
(p. 236)

Southern Blue Gum
(p. 238)

251

Index

PHOTOGRAPHS

Front cover photograph shows 'mixed woodland in autumn', © M J Thomas
(FLPA)

Photographs by Andreas Riedmiller except for:
  Aas: 50, 95 (below), 142 (right above); Cleave: 86 (left), 158 (below); Kalt: 75
(above), 215 (below); Kastro: 177 (above); Pott: 229 (above); Reinhard: 199
(below), 237; Schacht: 229 (below); Scherz: 43 (below), 69 (below), 104 (right
below), 169 (above), 171 (below); Schimmitat/Angerer: 122 (below); Sterry: 52
(left); Walters: 52 (right), 53, 87, 94, 122 (above), 123 (above), 131 (right
above), 136 (below), 147, 152, 158 (below), 191, 224 (above); Wildlife Matters:
69 (above), 95 (above), 183; Zauner: 128 (left above), 144 (right), 164 (right
below), 187; Zettl: 192 (right below).

Collins Nature Guides

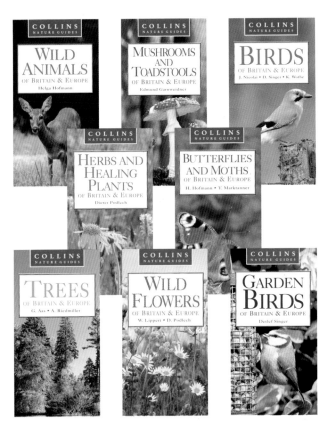

To order your copies please call our
24-hour credit card hotline 0141 772 2281

HarperCollins*Publishers*

Deciduous trees – silhouettes

Sycamore

Wych Elm

Apple

Pear

Rowan

Lime

Horse Chestnut